SAY IT IN
FRENCH
NEW EDITION

JENNIFER WAGNER

DOVER PUBLICATIONS, INC.
Mineola, New York

Bibliographical Note

Say It in French: New Edition, first published in 2011 by Dover Publications, Inc., is a completely revised and updated work, which supersedes the book of the same title originally published in 1950 and revised in 1962.

Library of Congress Cataloging-in-Publication Data

Wagner, Jennifer, 1982–
Say it in French / Jennifer Wagner. — New ed.
    p.   cm. —(Dover language guides)
Revised ed. of: Say It in French, 1950 by Dover.
Includes index.
ISBN-13: 978-0-486-47635-3
ISBN-10: 0-486-47635-9
1. French language—Pronunciation. 2. French language—Conversation and phrase books. I. Title.
PC2137.W24   2011
448.3'421—dc22
                    2011010699

Manufactured in the United States by Courier Corporation
47635901
www.doverpublications.com

Contents

CONTENTS

CONTENTS

Quick & to the Point/Sidebars

Throughout the book, you will notice two types of shaded boxes. The "Quick & to the Point" sections summarize the most important words and phrases contained in the chapter. These essential and handy phrases provide the easiest and simplest communication that a traveler may need on any given topic. The sidebars, also appearing in tinted boxes, contain an interesting fact for the traveler. Pertinent to the theme of each chapter, the sidebars may inform readers about a unique aspect of the culture, feature special details about the language, or offer a bit of entertaining trivia.

Introduction

PRONUNCIATION

The difficulties of pronunciation of French for an American arise mainly from the difference in the pronunciation of vowels. English vowels are usually not one sound, but two; French vowels are pure, consisting of one sound only. Remember not to drawl them, as in English.

The pronunciation given should be read simply as in English, with the stress placed slightly at the end of each word or group of words. Since in some cases the pronunciation of a group of letters differs according to the English word in which it is found and since a few French sounds cannot be represented in English, the following rules should be remembered:

ah—as in *father*

ay—as in *say*

aw—as in *saw*

ee—as in *bee*

eh—as the e in *let*

ew—pucker your lips and say *ee*; this sound is similar to the English word *dew*

g—always hard as in *go*

INTRODUCTION

zh—always soft as in *pleasure*

oh—as in *blow*

r—the French r is the sound made when one gargles

s—always as in *sister*

uh—as in *cup*

y—as in *yes* (when followed by a vowel)

y—as in *my* (when preceded by a consonant)

The English vowels found in the words *cat*, *did*, and *put* do not exist in French. The nasal sounds *ahn*, *awn*, *ehn*, and *uhn* are not fully pronounced through the mouth, but rather through the nose. Try pronouncing these syllables a few times while holding your nose. Be sure not to pronounce the *n* when it is underscored.

Another feature of French pronunciation that can be tricky for Americans is the liaison between words. Many times the final consonant sound of a word transfers to the beginning of the next word if the latter begins with a vowel. Sometimes this will force the pronunciation of a previously silent consonant, such as in *vous avez*. Independently, *vous* is pronounced "voo" and avez is pronounced "ah-vay," but together they are pronounced as "voo zah-vay."

INFORMAL AND FORMAL

French has two different ways to say "you," depending on whether the speaker wants to be informal (*tu*) or formal (*vous*). As a tourist, you will most likely only need to use the formal *vous* form, but you will hear the informal *tu* form in everyday speech. The general rule is to use *tu* with family members, close friends, children, and animals. *Vous* should be used with everyone else, and especially to show respect. Accidental use of *tu* with a stranger can be seen as an insult in Europe; however, the informal *tu* form is much more common in Quebec.

MASCULINE AND FEMININE

French also has masculine and feminine genders assigned to nouns and adjectives. In most cases, one adds an -e to the masculine word to form the feminine, unless the masculine already ends in an -e, in which case the masculine and feminine forms are identical. In many cases, the addition of -e changes only the spelling and not the pronunciation of the word. In cases where the pronunciation does differ between masculine and feminine forms, both pronunciations are given.

LA FRANCOPHONIE

In addition to France, this book includes the vocabulary of other French-speaking countries where the standard vocabulary may differ from French spoken in France, including:

- Belgium—the southern region called Wallonia;
- Switzerland—the cantons of Fribourg, Geneva, Jura, Neuchâtel, Valais, and Vaud; and

3

- Canada—the province of Quebec and the region of Acadia, which generally includes the Maritime provinces of New Brunswick, Nova Scotia and Prince Edward Island.

EVERYDAY EXPRESSIONS

Useful Phrases / *Des Expressions Utiles*

1. **Hello. Good-bye.**   Bonjour. Au revoir.
   bawn-ZHOOR. awr-VWAHR

2. **Good morning. Good evening.**   Bonjour. Bonsoir.
   bawn-ZHOOR. bawn-SWAHR

3. **Good night.** *(going to bed)*   Bonne nuit.   *bun NWEE*

4. **Hi / Bye.**   Salut.   *sah-LEW*

5. **See you soon. See you later.**
   À bientôt. À plus tard.   *ah byehn-TOH. ah plew TAHR*

6. **See you tonight. See you tomorrow.**
   À ce soir. À demain.   *ah suh SWAHR. ah duh-MEHN*

7. **Yes. No. Maybe.**   Oui. Non. Peut-être.
   wee. nawn. puh-TEH-truh

8. **Please. Thank you (very much).**
   S'il vous plaît. Merci (beaucoup).
   seel voo PLEH. mehr-SEE (boh-KOO)

9. **You're welcome.**
   Je vous en prie. / Bienvenue (Quebec).
   zhuh voo zahn PREE. / byehn-vuh-NEW

10. You're welcome. *(informal)*   De rien.
duh RYEHN

11. Excuse me. Pardon me.   Excusez-moi. Pardon.
ehk-SKEW-zay-MWAH. par-DAWN

12. Do you speak English?   Parlez-vous anglais?
par-lay-VOO ahn-GLEH

13. Does anyone here speak English?
Il y a quelqu'un ici qui parle anglais?
eel-YAH kehl-KUH nee-SEE kee parl ahn-GLEH

14. I speak only English.   Je parle seulement anglais.
zhuh parl SUHL-mahn ahn-GLEH

15. I don't speak French very well.
Je ne parle pas très bien français.
zhuh nuh parl pah treh byehn frahn-SEH

16. I speak a little French.   Je parle un peu français.
zhuh parl uhn puh frahn-SEH

17. German. Spanish. Italian.
Allemand. Espagnol. Italien.
al-MAHN. eh-spahn-YOL. ee-tah-LYEHN

18. Please speak more slowly.
Veuillez parler plus lentement.
vuh-yay par-lay plew lahn-tuh-MAHN

19. I (do not) understand.   Je (ne) comprends (pas).
zhuh (nuh) kawn-PRAHN (pah)

20. Repeat it, please.   Répétez-le, s'il vous plaît.
ray-pay-tay-LUH, seel voo PLEH

5

21. Write it down, please. Écrivez-le, s'il vous plaît.
ay-kree-vay-LUH, seel voo PLEH

22. What does it mean? Qu'est-ce que ça veut dire?
KEHS-kuh sah vuh DEER

23. How do you say ___ in French?
Comment dit-on ___ en français?
kaw-mahn dee-tawn ___ ahn frahn-SEH

24. How do you spell ___?
Comment écrivez-vous ___?
kaw-MAHN tay-KREE-vay-voo

25. Can you help me? Pouvez-vous m'aider?
poo-vay-voo may-DAY

26. I am looking for ___. Je cherche ___.
zhuh shehrsh

27. What do you want? Que voulez-vous?
KUH voo-lay-VOO

28. How much is it? Combien est-ce?
kawn-BYEHN ehss

29. Why? Pourquoi? *poor-KWAH*

30. When? Quand? *kahn*

31. Who? Qui? *kee*

32. What? Quoi? *kwah*

33. Where? Où? *oo*

34. How? Comment? *kaw-MAHN*

35. How long? Combien de temps?
kawn-BYEHN duh TAHN

36. How far? À quelle distance? *ah kehl dees-TAHNS*

37. Come here. Come in. Venez ici. Entrez.
vuh-nay zee-SEE. ahn-TRAY

38. Wait a moment. Attendez un moment.
ah-tahn-DAY uhn maw-MAHN

39. Have a nice day (evening).
Bonne journée (soirée). *bun zhoor-NAY (swa-RAY)*

40. Where is (are) ___? Où est (sont) ___?
oo eh (sawn)

41. Toilets. Toilettes. *twah-LEHT*

42. Men. Women. Hommes. Femmes. *awm. fahm*

43. Open. Closed. Ouvert. Fermé.
ooh-VEHR. fehr-MAY

44. Push. Pull. Pousser. Tirer. *POO-say. TEE-ray*

45. Entrance. Exit. Entrée. Sortie.
ahn-TRAY. sawr-TEE

46. Vacancy. No vacancy. Chambre Libre. Complet.
SHAHN-bruh LEE-bruh. kawn-PLEH

47. Information. Renseignements.
rahn-SEHN-yuh-mahn

48. Forbidden. Interdit. *ehn-tehr-DEE*

49. Out of Order. Hors Service. *awr sehr-VEESS*

50. Here. There. Over there. Ici. Là. Là-bas.
ee-SEE. lah. lah-BAH

51. I am (not) in a hurry. Je (ne) suis (pas) pressé(e).
zhuh (nuh) swee (pah) preh-SAY

7

52. I am warm / cold. J'ai chaud / froid.
zhay SHOH / FRWAH

53. I am hungry / thirsty / sleepy.
J'ai faim / soif / sommeil.
zhay FEHN / SWAHF / saw-MAY

54. I am busy / tired / ill.
Je suis occupé(e) / fatigué(e) / malade.
zhuh swee zaw-kew-PAY / fah-tee-GAY / mah-LAD

55. I am lost / late. Je suis perdu(e) / en retard.
zhuh swee pehr-DEW / awn ruh-TAHR

56. It is (it is not) all right. C'est (ce n'est pas) bien.
seh (suh neh pah) BYEHN

57. It is old / new. C'est vieux / nouveau.
seh VYUH / noo-VOH

58. That is (that is not) all. C'est (ce n'est pas) tout.
seh (suh neh pah) TOO

59. Empty. Full. Vide. Plein. *veed. plehn*

60. Again. Also. Encore. Aussi. *ahn-KAWR. oh-SEE*

61. To. From. With. À. De. Avec. *ah. duh. ah-VEHK*

62. In. On. Near. Far from. Dans. Sur. Près de. Loin de.
dahn. sewr. PREH duh. LWEHN duh

63. In front of. Behind. Devant. Derrière.
duh-VAHN. deh-RYEHR

64. Beside. Inside. Outside.
À côté. À l'intérieur. À l'extérieur. *ah koh-TAY.*
ah lehn-tay-RYUHR. ah lehk-stay-RYUHR

65. Something. Nothing.   Quelque chose. Rien.
kehl-kuh SHOHZ. ryehn

66. Several. Few.   Plusieurs. Quelques.
plew-ZYUHR. kehl-kuh

67. (Much) more, less.   (Beaucoup) plus, moins.
(boh-koo) plew, mwehn

68. (A little) more, less.   (Un peu) plus, moins.
(uhn PUH) plew, mwehn

69. Enough. Too much.   Assez. Trop.   *ah-SAY. troh.*

70. Much. Many.   Beaucoup. Beaucoup.
boh-KOO. boh-KOO.

71. Good. Better (than).   Bon. Meilleur (que).
bawn. may-YUHR (kuh)

72. Bad. Worse (than).   Mauvais. Pire (que).
moh-VEH. peer (kuh)

73. Now. Immediately.   Maintenant. Tout de suite.
mehnt-NAHN. toot SWEET

74. Soon. Later.   Bientôt. Plus tard.
byehn-TOH. plew TAHR

75. As soon as possible.   Aussitôt que possible.
oh-see-TOH kuh paw-SEE-bluh

76. At the latest. At least.   Au plus tard. Au moins.
oh plew TAHR. oh MWEHN

77. It is (too) late.   C'est (trop) tard.   *seh (troh) TAHR*

78. It is early.   C'est tôt.   *seh TOH*

79. **Slowly. Slower.**   Lentement. Plus lentement.
lahnt-MAHN. plew lahnt-MAHN

80. **Quickly. Faster.**   Vite. Plus vite.   *veet. plew veet.*

81. **What is the matter?**   Qu'est-ce qu'il y a?
kehs-keel-YAH

82. **It's OK.**   Ça va.   *sah vah*

83. **It's not serious.**   Ce n'est pas grave.
suh neh pah GRAHV

84. **It doesn't matter.**   Ça ne fait rien.
sah nuh feh RYEHN

85. **Listen. Look here.**   Écoutez. Regardez.
ay-koo-TAY. ruh-gar-DAY

86. **I would like ___.**   Je voudrais ___.
zhuh voo-DREH

87. **Can you recommend a ___?**
Pouvez-vous me recommander un ___?
poo-vay-voo muh ruh-kaw-mahn-DAY uhn

88. **Do you want ___?**   Voulez-vous ___?
voo-lay-voo

89. **I am glad.**   J'en suis content (contente).
zhahn swee kawn-TAHN (kawn-TAHNT)

90. **I am sorry.**   Je suis désolé(e).
zhuh swee DAY-zoh-lay

91. **It is (it is not) my fault.**
C'est (ce n'est pas) ma faute.
seh (suh neh pah) mah FOHT

Quick & to the Point

Useful Phrases / Des Expressions Utiles

May I introduce Mr. (Mrs., Miss) ____?
Puis-je présenter Monsieur (Madame, Mademoiselle) ____?
PWEE-zhuh pray-zahn-tay muh-SYUH (ma-DAHM, mad-mwah-ZEHL)

This is ____.
Je vous présente ____.
zhuh voo pray-ZAHNT

What is your name?
Comment vous appelez-vous?
kaw-MAHN voo zahp-play-VOO

My name is ____.
Je m'appelle ____.
zhuh mah-PEHL

Nice to meet you.
Enchanté(e).
ahn-shahn-TAY

How are you? (formal)
Comment allez-vous?
kaw-mahn tah-lay-VOO

Fine, thanks. And you? (formal)
Très bien, merci. Et vous?
treh BYEHN, mehr-SEE. eh VOO

How are you? (informal)   Ça va?   *sah vah*

All right. And you? (informal)
Ça va. Et toi?
sah va. eh TWAH

11

EVERYDAY EXPRESSIONS

92. **Whose fault is it?** À qui la faute? *ah kee la FOHT*

93. **I (do not) know.** Je (ne) sais (pas).
zhuh (nuh) say (pah)

94. **I (do not) think so.** Je (ne) le crois (pas).
zhuh (nuh) luh krwah (pah)

95. **What is that used for?** À quoi ça sert-il?
ah KWAH sah sehr-TEEL

Introductions / Les Présentations

96. **My wife. My husband.** Ma femme. Mon mari.
ma FAHM. mawn ma-REE

97. **My spouse/partner.** (male) Mon conjoint. /
(female) Ma conjointe.
mawn kohn-ZHWAHN / mah kohn-ZHWAHNT

98. **My boyfriend. My girlfriend.**
Mon copain. Ma copine.
mawn koh-PEHN. mah koh-PEEN
Mon chum. Ma blonde (Quebec).
mawn CHUHM. mah BLAWND

99. **My family. My children.** Ma famille. Mes enfants.
mah fah-MEE. meh zahn-FAHN

100. **My daughter. My son.** Ma fille. Mon fils.
ma FEE-uh. mawn FEESS

101. **My friend. My colleague.**
Mon ami(e). Mon/Ma collègue.
maw na-MEE. mawn/mah kaw-LEHG

102. My sister. My brother.   Ma sœur. Mon frère.
ma SUHR. mawn FREHR

103. How nice to see you again.
Quel plaisir de vous revoir.
kehl pleh-ZEER duh voo ruh-VWAHR

104. How is your family?   Comment va votre famille?
kaw-mahn vah vaw-truh fah-MEE

105. (Not) very well.   (Pas) très bien.   *(pah) treh byehn*

106. Please sit down. *(formal)*   Veuillez vous asseoir.
vuh-yay voo zah-SWAHR

107. Please sit down. *(informal)*   Assieds-toi.
ah-syay-TWAH

108. Make yourself at home. *(formal)*
Faites comme chez vous.   *feht kawm shay VOO*

109. Make yourself at home. *(informal)*
Fais comme chez toi.   *feh kawm shay TWAH*

110. I am here on business.
Je suis ici en voyage d'affaires.
zhuh swee zee-SEE ahn vwah-YAHZH dah-FEHR

111. I am on vacation.   Je suis en vacances.
zhuh swee zahn vah-KAHNS

112. I had a good time.   Je me suis trés bien amusé(e).
zhuh muh swee treh byeh nah-mew-ZAY

113. I hope to see you again soon.
J'espère vous revoir bientôt.
zhess-PEHR voo ruh-VWAHR byehn-TOH

114. Come see me (us).   Venez me (nous) voir.
vuh-nay muh (noo) VWAHR

115. Give me your address (and telephone number).
Donnez-moi votre adresse (et votre numéro de
téléphone).
*daw-nay-MWAH vaw-trah-DREHSS (ay VAW-truh
new-may-ROH duh tay-lay-FAWN)*

116. My (e-mail) address is . . .
Mon adresse (e-mail) est . . .
maw na-DREHSS (ee-MEHL) eh

117. Give my regards to . . .   Mes amitiés à . . .
may za-mee-TYAY zah

118. We are traveling to . . .   Nous voyageons à . . .
noo vwah-ya-ZHAWN za

Social Phrases / Des Expressions Sociales

119. I'm married / divorced.
Je suis marié(e) / divorcé(e).
zhuh swee mah-ree-AY / dee-vawr-SAY

120. I'm single / separated.
Je suis célibataire / séparé(e).
zhuh swee say-lee-bah-TEHR / say-pah-RAY

121. I'm in a civil union with my partner. (officially
recognized by the state)
Je suis PACSé avec mon/ma conjoint(e). (France,
Switzerland)
*zhuh swee pahk-SAY ah-VEHK mawn/mah
kawn-ZHWAHN(T)*

122. Where are you from? (*formal*)   D'où venez-vous?
DOO vuh-nay-VOO

123. Where are you from? (*informal*)   Tu viens d'où?
tew vyeh<u>n</u> DOO

124. I am from the United States / Canada.
Je viens des États-Unis / du Canada.
zhuh vyeh<u>n</u> day zay-TA-zew-NEE / dew kah-nah-DAH

125. I am from Chicago / Toronto.
Je suis de Chicago / Toronto.
zhuh swee duh shee-kah-GOH / toh-rawn-TOH

126. I am American.   Je suis américain / américaine.
zhuh swee zah-may-ree-KEH<u>N</u> / zah-may-ree-KEHNN

127. I am Canadian.   Je suis canadien / canadienne.
zhuh swee kah-nah-DYEH<u>N</u> / kah-nah-DYEHNN

128. I am from Quebec.   Je suis québécois / québécoise.
zhuh swee kay-bay-KWAH / kay-bay-KWAHZ

129. Are you French? (*formal*)
Êtes-vous français / française?
eht-voo frah<u>n</u>-SEH / frah<u>n</u>-SEHZ

130. Are you Belgian / Swiss? (*informal*)
Tu es belge / suisse?
tew eh BEHLZH / SWEESS

131. How old are you?   Quel âge avez-vous?
kehl AHZH ah-vay-voo

132. I am 30 years old.   J'ai trente ans.
zhay TRAH<u>N</u>T ahn

133. How long have you been here?
Depuis quand êtes-vous ici?
duh-pwee KAHN eht-voo zee-SEE

134. I've been here ___ days/weeks.
Je suis ici depuis ___ jours/semaines.
zhuh swee zee-see duh-pwee ___ ZHOOR/suh-MEHNN

135. What do you do for a living?
Qu'est-ce que vous faites dans la vie?
kehs-kuh voo FEHT dahn lah VEE

136. What is your line of work?
Quelle est votre profession?
kehl eh vaw-truh praw-fehs-SYAWN

137. I am ___. Je suis ___. *zhuh swee*

138. . . . a teacher/a professor. . . . professeur.
prawf-SUHR

139. . . . a doctor. . . . médecin. *mayd-SEHN*

140. . . . a dentist. . . . dentiste. *dahn-TEEST*

141. . . . an accountant. . . . comptable.
kawn-TAH-bluh

142. . . . an engineer. . . . ingénieur/ingénieure.
ehn-zhay-NYUHR

143. . . . an architect. . . . architecte. *ar-shee-TEHKT*

144. . . . a lawyer. . . . avocat/avocate.
ah-voh-KAH/ah-voh-KAHT

145. . . . a journalist. . . . journaliste. *zhoor-nah-LEEST*

146. . . . a civil servant. . . . fonctionnaire.
fawnk-syaw-NEHR

16

147. ... **a blue-collar employee.** ... ouvrier / ouvrière.
oov-RYAY / oov-RYEHR

148. ... **a stay-at-home mom.** ... femme au foyer.
fahm oh fwah-YAY

149. ... **a stay-at-home dad.** ... homme au foyer.
awm oh fwah-YAY

150. I am retired / unemployed.
Je suis à la retraite / au chômage.
zhuh swee zah lah ruh-TREHT / zoh shoh-MAHZH

151. I am a university student.
Je suis étudiant / étudiante.
zhuh swee zay-tew-DYAHN / zay-tew-DYAHNT

152. I study ___. J'étudie ___. *zhay-tew-dee*

153. ... **English.** ... l'anglais. *lahn-GLEH*

154. ... **French.** ... le français. *luh frahn-SEH*

155. ... **literature.** ... la littérature.
la lee-tay-rah-TEWR

156. ... **psychology.** ... la psychologie.
la psee-kaw-law-ZHEE

157. ... **history.** ... l'histoire. *lees-TWAHR*

158. ... **geography.** ... la géographie.
lah zhay-oh-grah-FEE

159. ... **biology.** ... la biologie. *lah byaw-law-ZHEE*

160. ... **chemistry.** ... la chimie. *lah shee-MEE*

161. ... **engineering.** ... l'ingénierie.
lehn-zhay-nee-REE

17

162. . . . **math.** . . . les mathématiques.
lay mah-tay-mah-TEEK

163. . . . **accounting.** . . . le comptabilité.
luh kawn-tah-bee-lee-TEH

164. . . . **computer science.** . . . l'informatique.
leh<u>n</u>-fawr-mah-TEEK

165. . . . **political science.** . . . les sciences politiques.
lay see-AH<u>N</u>S paw-lee-TEEK

166. I am doing a Bachelor's degree.
Je fais une licence / un baccalauréat (Quebec).
zhuh feh ewn lee-SAH<u>N</u>S / uh<u>n</u> bah-kah-law-ray-AH

167. I am doing a Master's degree.
Je fais un master / une maîtrise (Quebec).
zhuh feh uh<u>n</u> mah-STEHR / ewn meh-TREEZ

168. I am doing a Ph.D. / a post-doctoral fellowship.
Je fais un doctorat / un stage postdoctoral.
zhuh feh uh<u>n</u> dawk-taw-RAH / uh<u>n</u> STAHZH pawst-dawk-taw-RAHL

Describing People / *Décrire les Gens*

169. What does he / she look like?
Comment est-il / elle?   *kaw-mah<u>n</u> eh-TEEL / EHL*

170. Can you describe her?   Pouvez-vous la décrire?
poo-vay-VOO lah day-KREER

171. He is young / old / handsome / ugly.
Il est jeune / vieux / beau / laid.
eel eh zhuhn / vyuh / boh / leh

172. She is young / old / beautiful / ugly.
Elle est jeune / vieille / belle / laide.
ehl eh zhuhn / vyay / behl / lehd

173. I am tall / short / medium height.
Je suis grand(e) / petit(e) / de taille moyenne.
*zhuh swee GRAHN(D) / puh-TEE(T) / duh TY-uh
mwah-YEHNN*

174. I am thin / fat / tan / pale.
Je suis mince / gros(se) / bronzé(e) / pâle.
zhuh swee mehns / groh(s) / brawn-ZAY / pahl

175. He has blue / brown / green / hazel eyes.
Il a les yeux bleus / marron / verts / noisette.
eel ah lay zyuh bluh / mah-RAWN / vehr / nwah-ZEHT

176. She has blond / red / gray hair.
Elle a les cheveux blonds / roux / gris.
ehl ah lay shuh-vuh blawn / rooh / gree

177. He has brown / chestnut brown / black hair.
Il a les cheveux bruns / châtain / noirs.
eel ah lay shuh-vuh bruhn / sha-TEHN / nwahr

178. She has short / long / straight / curly hair.
Elle a les cheveux courts / longs / raides / bouclés.
ehl ah lay shuh-vuh koor / lawn / rehd / boo-KLAY

179. She has freckles / a beauty mark.
Elle a des taches de rousseur / un grain de beauté.
*ehl ah day tahsh duh roo-SUHR / uhn grehn duh
boh-TAY*

19

180. **He has a beard / a mustache.**
Il porte une barbe / une moustache.
eel pawrt ewn BAHRB / ewn moo-STAHSH

181. **He is bald.**   Il est chauve.   *eel eh SHOHV*

182. **He has a tattoo / a piercing.**
Il a un tatouage / un piercing.
eel ah uhn tah-TWAHZH / uhn peer-SEENG

183. **She wears glasses / braces.**
Elle porte des lunettes / un appareil dentaire.
ehl pawrt day lew-NEHT / uh nah-pah-RAY dahn-TEHR

184. **I am 1.60 meters tall.**   Je mesure 1 mètre 60.
zhuh meh-ZEWR uhn meh-truh swah-SAHNT

185. **I weigh 55 kilos.**   Je pèse 55 kilos.
zhuh pehz sehn-kahnt-SEHNK kee-LOH

186. **You are ___.** *(formal)*   Vous êtes ___.   *voo zeht*

187. **. . . nice.**   . . . gentil / gentille.
zhahn-TEE / zhahn-TEE-yuh

188. **. . . cute.**   . . . mignon / mignonne.
meen-YAWN / meen-YAWNN

189. **. . . intelligent.**   . . . intelligent / intelligente.
ehn-teh-lee-ZHAHN / ehn-teh-lee-ZHAHNT

190. **. . . funny.**   . . . drôle.   *drohl*

191. **. . . serious.**   . . . sérieux / sérieuse.
say-RYUH / say-RYUHZ

192. **. . . mean.**   . . . méchant / méchante.
may-SHAHN / may-SHAHNT

193. . . . **rude.** . . . impoli / impolie. *ehn-poh-LEE*

194. You seem ___. *(informal)* Tu as l'air ___.
tew ah lehr

195. . . . **happy.** . . . heureux / heureuse.
uh-RUH / uh-RUHZ

196. . . . **sad.** . . . triste. *treest*

197. . . . **depressed.** . . . déprimé / déprimée.
day-pree-MAY

198. . . . **calm.** . . . calme. *kahlm*

199. . . . **clever.** . . . malin / maligne.
mah-LEH<u>N</u> / mah-LEEN-yuh

Difficulties / *Les Difficultés*

200. I cannot find my hotel address.
Je ne peux pas trouver l'adresse de mon hôtel.
zhuh nuh puh pah troo-vay lah-DREHS duh maw
noh-TEHL

201. I do not remember the street.
Je ne me rappelle pas la rue.
zhuh nuh muh rah-pehl pah la REW

202. I have lost my friends. J'ai perdu mes amis.
zhay pehr-DEW meh zah-MEE

203. I left my purse (wallet) in the ___.
J'ai laissé mon sac (portefeuille) dans le ___.
zhay leh-say maw<u>n</u> SAK (pawr-tuh-FUH-yuh) dah<u>n</u> luh

21

EVERYDAY EXPRESSIONS

204. I forgot my money (my keys).
J'ai oublié mon argent (mes clés).
zhay oo-blee-AY maw nar-ZHAHN (may KLAY)

205. I have missed my train (plane, bus).
J'ai manqué mon train (avion, bus).
zhay mahn-kay mawn TREHN (av-YAWN, BEWS)

206. What should I do?   Que dois-je faire?
kuh DWAH-zhuh FEHR

207. You said it would cost ___.
Vous avez dit qu'il coûterait ___.
voo zah-vay DEE keel koot-REH

208. They are bothering me.   Ils m'ennuient.
eel mahn-NWEE

209. I'm going to call the police.
Je vais appeler la police.
zhuh vay zah-PLAY la paw-LEESS

210. Where is the police station?
Où est le commissariat de police?
oo eh luh kaw-mee-sa-RYAH duh paw-LEESS

211. I have been robbed of ___.   On m'a volé ___.
awn ma vaw-lay

212. The lost and found desk.
Le bureau des objets trouvés.
luh bew-ROH day zawb-zheh troo-VAY

213. Help!   Au secours!   *oh suh-KOOR*

214. Thief!   Au voleur!   *oh vaw-LUHR*

215. Fire!   Au feu!   *oh FUH*

Emergency Phone Numbers /
Les numéros d'urgence

112 is the free emergency telephone number to reach the police, ambulances, and fire departments throughout the European Union and Switzerland. However, many countries still have their own emergency numbers:

	Belgium	France	Switzerland
Police	101	17	117
Ambulance	100	15	144
Fire Dept.	100	18	118

Canada uses 911, just as in the United States.

216. Look out! Attention! *ah-tahn-SYAWN*

217. Leave me alone! Laissez-moi tranquille!
lehs-say-mwah trahn-KEEL

218. Go away! Allez-vous-en! *ah-lay-voo-ZAHN*

NUMBERS AND TIME

Cardinal Numbers / *Les Nombres Cardinaux*

219. One. Un. *uhn*

220. Two. Deux. *duh*

221. Three. Trois. *trwah*

222. Four. Quatre. *KAH-truh*

223. Five. Cinq. *sehnk*

224. Six. Six. *seess*

225. Seven. Sept. *seht*

226. Eight. Huit. *weet*

227. Nine. Neuf. *nuhf*

228. Ten. Dix. *deess*

229. Eleven. Onze. *awnz*

230. Twelve. Douze. *dooz*

231. Thirteen. Treize. *trehz*

232. Fourteen. Quatorze. *kah-TAWRZ*

233. Fifteen. Quinze. *kehnz*

234. Sixteen. Seize. *sehz*

235. Seventeen. Dix-sept. *dee-SEHT*

236. Eighteen. Dix-huit. *dee-ZWEET*

237. Nineteen. Dix-neuf. *dee-ZNUHF*

238. Twenty. Vingt. *vehn*

239. Twenty-one. Vingt-et-un. *vehn-tay-UHN*

240. Twenty-two. Vingt-deux. *vehn-DUH*

241. Twenty-three. Vingt-trois. *vehn-TRWAH*

242. Twenty-four. Vingt-quatre. *vehn-KAH-truh*

243. Twenty-five. Vingt-cinq. *vehnt-SEHNK*

244. Twenty-six. Vingt-six. *vehn-SEESS*

245. Twenty-seven. Vingt-sept. *vehn-SEHT*

246. Twenty-eight. Vingt-huit. *vehn-TWEET*

247. Twenty-nine. Vingt-neuf. *vehn-NUHF*

248. Thirty. Trente. *trahnt*

249. Thirty-one. Trente et un. *trahn tay UHN*

250. Thirty-two. Trente-deux. *trahn-DUH*

251. Thirty-three. Trente-trois. *trahn-TRWAH*

252. Forty. Quarante. *kah-RAHNT*

253. Fifty. Cinquante. *sehn-KAHNT.*

254. Sixty. Soixante. *swah-SAHNT*

255. Seventy.
Soixante-dix (France and Quebec). *swah-sahnt-DEESS*
Septante (Acadia, Belgium, and Switzerland).
seh-TAHNT

256. Seventy-one. Soixante-et-onze (France and
Quebec). *swah-sahn-tay-AWNZ*
Septante et un (Acadia, Belgium, and Switzerland).
seh-tahn tay-UHN

257. Seventy-two.
Soixante-douze (France and Quebec).
swah-sahnt-DOOZ
Septante-deux (Acadia, Belgium, and Switzerland).
seh-tahnt-DUH

25

258. Eighty. Quatre-vingts (France, Belgium, and Quebec).
kah-truh-VEHN Huitante (Switzerland: Fribourg,
Valais, Vaud). *wee-TAHNT*

259. Eighty-one.
Quatre-vingt-un (France, Belgium, and Quebec).
kah-truh-vehn-UHN
Huitante-et-un (Switzerland: Fribourg, Valais, Vaud).
wee-tahn-tay-UHN

260. Eighty-two.
Quatre-vingt-deux (France, Belgium, and Quebec).
kah-truh-vehn-DUH
Huitante-deux (Switzerland: Fribourg, Valais, Vaud).
wee-tahnt-DUH

261. Ninety. Quatre-vingt-dix (France and Quebec).
kah-truh-vehn-DEESS
Nonante (Acadia, Belgium, and Switzerland).
naw-NAHNT

262. Ninety-one.
Quatre-vingt-onze (France and Quebec).
kah-truh-vehn-AWNZ
Nonante-et-un (Acadia, Belgium, and Switzerland).
naw-nahn-tay-UHN

263. Ninety-two.
Quatre-vingt-douze (France and Quebec).
kah-truh-vehn-DOOZ
Nonante-deux (Acadia, Belgium, and Switzerland).
naw-nahnt-DUH

264. One hundred. Cent. *sahn*

265. **One hundred one.** Cent un. *sahn-UHN*

266. **Two hundred.** Deux cents. *DUH sahn*

267. **One thousand.** Mille. *meel*

268. **One thousand one.** Mille-un. *meel-UHN*

269. **Two thousand.** Deux-mille. *DUH meel*

270. **Million.** Un million. *uhn meel-YAWN*

271. **Billion.** Un milliard. *uhn meel-YAHR*

Ordinal Numbers / Les Nombres Ordinaux

272. **First.** Premier / Première.
pruh-MYAY / pruh-MYEHR

273. **Second.** Deuxième. *DUH-zyehm*

274. **Third.** Troisième. *TRWAH-zyehm*

275. **Fourth.** Quatrième. *KAH-tryehm*

276. **Fifth.** Cinquième. *SEHN-kyehm*

277. **Sixth.** Sixième. *SEE-zyehm*

278. **Seventh.** Septième. *SEH-tyehm*

279. **Eighth.** Huitième. *WEE-tyehm*

280. **Ninth.** Neuvième. *NUH-vyehm*

281. **Tenth.** Dixième. *DEE-zyehm*

282. **Eleventh.** Onzième. *AWN-zyehm*

283. **Twelfth.** Douzième. *DOO-zyehm*

284. **Thirteenth.** Treizième. *TREH-zyehm*

285. **Fourteenth.** Quatorzième. *kah-TAWR-zyehm*

286. **Fifteenth.**   Quinzième.   *KEHN-zyehm*

287. **Sixteenth.**   Seizième.   *SEH-zyehm*

288. **Seventeenth.**   Dix-septième.   *dee-SEH-tyehm*

289. **Eighteenth.**   Dix-huitième.   *dee-ZWEE-tyehm*

290. **Nineteenth.**   Dix-neuvième.   *dee-ZNUH-vyehm*

291. **Twentieth.**   Vingtième.   *VEHN-tyehm*

292. **Twenty-first.**   Vingt-et-unième.
vehn-tay-EW-nyehm

293. **Twenty-second.**   Vingt-deuxième.
vehn-DUH-zyehm

294. **Twenty-third.**   Vingt-troisième.
vehn-TRWAH-zyehm

295. **Hundredth.**   Centième.   *SAHN-tyehm*

296. **1025.**   Mille-vingt-cinq.   *meel-vehn-SEHNK*

297. **1789.**   Mille-sept-cent-quatre-vingt-neuf.
meel-seht-sahn-kah-truh-vehn-NUHF

298. **1968.**   Mille-neuf-cent-soixante-huit.
meel-nuhf-sahn-swah-sahn-TWEET

299. **2010.**   Deux-mille-dix.   *duh-meel-DEESS*

Time / L'Heure

300. **What time is it?**   Quelle heure est-il?
keh LUHR eh-TEEL

301. **It's nine a.m.**   Il est neuf heures du matin.
eel eh NUH vuhr dew mah-TEHN

302. It's two p.m.   Il est deux heures de l'après-midi.
eel eh DUH zuhr duh lah-PREH-mee-DEE
Il est quatorze heures.
eel eh kah-TAWR zuhr

303. It's half past four.   Il est quatre heures et demie.
eel eh KAH truhr ay duh-MEE

304. It's a quarter past seven.
Il est sept heures et quart.
eel eh SEH tuhr ay KAHR

305. It's a quarter to four.
Il est quatre heures moins le quart.
eel eh KAH truhr mwehn luh KAHR

306. It's ten minutes past eight.   Il est huit heures dix.
eel eh WEE tuhr DEESS

307. It's ten minutes to five.
Il est cinq heures moins dix.
eel eh SEHN kuhr mwehn DEESS

308. Morning. In the morning.   Le matin. Du matin.
luh mah-TEHN. Dew mah-TEHN.

309. Evening. In the evening.   Le soir. Du soir.
luh swahr. dew swahr

310. Afternoon. In the afternoon.
L'après-midi. De l'après-midi.
lah-PREH-mee-DEE. Duh lah-PREH-mee-DEE.

311. At noon.   À midi.   *ah mee-DEE*

312. Midnight.   Minuit.   *mee-NWEE*

29

Quick & to the Point: Time / L'Heure

day	le jour	luh zhoor
night	la nuit	lah nwee
yesterday	hier	ee-YEHR
last night	hier soir	ee-yehr-SWAHR
today	aujourd'hui	oh-zhoor-DWEE
tonight	ce soir	suh swahr
tomorrow	demain	duh-MEHN
week	la semaine	lah suh-MEHNN
month	le mois	luh mwah
year	l'an	lahn

313. **The day before yesterday.** Avant-hier.
ah-vahn-TYEHR

314. **The day after tomorrow.** Après-demain.
ah-preh-duh-MEHN

315. **Weekend.**
Le week-end. / La fin de semaine (Quebec).
luh week-EHND. lah FEHN duh suh-MEHNN

316. **Decade.** La décennie. lah day-suh-NEE.

317. **Century.** Le siècle. luh SYEH-kluh.

318. **Millennium.** Le millénaire. luh mee-lay-NEHR.

319. **Last year.** L'année dernière.
lah-NAY dehr-NYEHR

320. **Last month.** Le mois passé. luh mwah pah-SAY

321. **Next Monday.** Lundi prochain. LUHN-dee
praw-SHEHN.

322. Next week.   La semaine prochaine.
lah suh-MEHNN praw-SHEHNN

323. Two weeks ago.   Il y a quinze jours.
eel-yah keh<u>n</u>z zhoor

324. One week ago.   Il y a huit jours.
eel-yah weet zhoor

Days and Months / *Les Jours et Les Mois*

325. Monday.   Lundi.   *LUH<u>N</u>-dee*

326. Tuesday.   Mardi.   *MAHR-dee*

327. Wednesday.   Mercredi.   *MEHR-kruh-dee*

328. Thursday.   Jeudi.   *ZHUH-dee*

329. Friday.   Vendredi.   *VAH<u>N</u>-druh-dee*

330. Saturday.   Samedi.   *SAHM-dee*

331. Sunday.   Dimanche.   *dee-MAH<u>N</u>SH*

332. January.   Janvier.   *ZHAH<u>N</u>-vyay*

333. February.   Février.   *FAYV-ryay*

334. March.   Mars.   *mahrs*

335. April.   Avril.   *ah-VREEL*

336. May.   Mai.   *meh*

337. June.   Juin.   *zhweh<u>n</u>*

338. July.   Juillet.   *ZHWEE-yeh*

339. August.   Août.   *oot*

340. September.   Septembre.   *sehp-TAH<u>N</u>-bruh*

341. October. Octobre. *awk-TAW-bruh*

342. November. Novembre. *naw-VAHN-bruh*

343. December. Décembre. *day-SAHN-bruh*

344. What day is today? On est quel jour aujourd'hui?
aw neh KEHL zhoor oh-zhoor-DWEE

345. Today is Tuesday. On est mardi.
aw neh MAHR-dee

346. When is your birthday?
Quelle est la date de votre anniversaire?
kehl eh la DAHT duh vaw trah-nee-vehr-SEHR

Time and Dates/ L'heure et les dates

The 24-hour clock is used throughout Europe for almost all schedules, including public transportation and plane schedules, as well as for work and school schedules. It is much more common to use quinze heures instead of trois heures de l'après-midi, for example. Note that you cannot use demi or quart when expressing time with the 24-hour clock — you must only use the cardinal numbers to refer to minutes.

Outside of the U.S. and Canada, the month/day/year format is rarely used to write dates. Instead, it is written day/month/year. European calendars also begin each week on Monday instead of Sunday.

347. My birthday is March 1.
Mon anniversaire est le premier mars.
maw nah-nee-vehr-SEHR eh luh pruh-myay MAHRS

348. My birthday is July 12.
Mon anniversaire est le 12 juillet.
maw nah-nee-vehr-SEHR eh luh dooz zhwee-YEH

Seasons and Weather / *Les Saisons and Le Temps*

349. Spring. Le printemps. *luh prehn-TAHN*

350. Summer. L'été. *lay-TAY*

351. Autumn. L'automne. *lohH-TAWN*

352. Winter. L'hiver. *lee-VEHR*

353. What's the weather like? Quel temps fait-il?
kehl tahn feh-TEEL

354. It's warm / cold. Il fait chaud / froid.
eel feh SHOH / FRWAH

355. It's nice / cool. Il fait bon / frais.
eel feh BAWN / FREH

356. It's good / bad out. Il fait beau / mauvais.
eel feh BOH / moh-VEH

357. It's raining. Il pleut. / Il mouille (Quebec).
eel PLUH / eel moo-EE-yuh

358. It's snowing. Il neige. *eel NEHZH*

359. It's hailing. Il grêle. *eel GREHL*

360. It's sunny / cloudy. Il fait soleil / nuageux.
eel feh soh-LAY / new-ah-ZHUH

361. It's windy / foggy.   Il fait du vent / du brouillard.
eel feh dew VAHN / dew broo-ee-YAHR

362. It's humid / mild.   Il fait humide / doux.
eel feh ew-MEED / DOO

363. It's boiling. / It's freezing. (*informal*)
On étouffe. / Ça caille.   *aw nay-TOOF / sah KAH-yuh*

TRAVEL AND TRANSPORTATION

Traveling / Voyager

364. I want to go to the airline office.
Je veux aller au bureau de la compagnie aérienne.
*zhuh vuh zal-lay oh bew-ROH de la kawn-pan-yee
ah-ay-ree-EHNN*

365. How long will it take to get to ___?
Combien de temps le voyage à ___ va-t-il durer?
*kawn-byehn duh TAHN luh vwah-yahzh ah ___
va-teel dew-RAY*

366. When will we arrive at ___?
Quand arriverons-nous à ___?
kahn tah-ree-vuh-rawn-noo ah

367. Please get me a taxi.
Appelez-moi un taxi, s'il vous plaît.
ah-play-MWAH uhn tak-SEE, seel voo pleh

368. The ticket office. The ticket machine.
Le guichet. Le guichet automatique.
luh ghee-SHEH. le ghee-sheh oh-taw-mah-TEEK

Quick & to the Point

Traveling / Voyager

Where is. . . ?	Où est. . . ?	ooh eh
the subway	le métro	luh may-TROH
the tramway	le tramway	luh trahm-WAY
the bus stop	l'arrêt de bus	lah-reh duh BEWSS
the railroad station	la gare (ferroviaire)	lah gar (fehr-oh-VYEHR)
the bus station	la gare routière	lah gar roo-TYEHR
the taxi stand	la station de taxis	lah sta-SYAWN duh tak-SEE
the dock	le quai	luh keh
the airport	l'aéroport	lah-ay-raw-PAWR
Is it far / near?	Est-ce loin / près d'ici?	ehs lwehn / preh dee SEE
To the right / left	À droite / à gauche	ah DRWAHT / ah GOHSH
Straight ahead	Tout droit	too drwah
To the north / south	Au nord / au sud	oh NAWR / oh SEWD
To the east / west	À l'est / à l'ouest	ah LEHST / ah LWEST

369. **A ticket. A timetable. The platform.**
Un billet. Un horaire. Le quai.
uhn bee-YEH. uh naw-RAYR. luh KEH

370. **The baggage room. The waiting room.**
La consigne. La salle d'attente.
lah kawn-SEEN-yuh. lah sahl dah-TAWNT

35

371. Is this seat taken?   Cette place est-elle prise?
seht plahss eh-tehl PREEZ

372. Can I reserve a seat?   Puis-je réserver une place?
PWEE-zhuh ray-zehr-vay ewn PLAHSS

373. A seat near the window (aisle).
Une place près de la fenêtre (du couloir).
ewn plahss preh duh la fuh-NEH-truh (dew koo-LWAHR)

374. Is this the (direct) way to ____?
Est-ce le chemin (direct) à ____?
ehs luh shuh-MEHN (dee-REKT) ah

375. How does one go (there)?   Comment va-t-on (là)?
kaw-MAHN va-tawn (LAH)

376. Where do I turn?   Où dois-je tourner?
oo dwah-zhuh toor-NAY

377. Forward. Back.   En avant. En arrière.
ah nah-VAHN. ah na-ree-EHR

378. Street. Place (Square).   Rue. Place.   *rew. plahss*

379. Am I going in the right direction?
Est-ce la bonne direction?
ehs la bawn dee-rek-SYAWN

380. Can you point?
Voulez-vous me le montrer du doigt?
voo-lay-voo muh luh mawn-tray dew DWAH

381. What street is this?   Quelle est cette rue?
keh leh seht REW

382. Where is the city center?   Où est le centre-ville?
ooh eh luh sah<u>n</u>-truh-VEEL

383. Do I have to change?   Dois-je changer?
dwah-zhuh shah<u>n</u>-ZHAY

384. Please tell me where to get off.
Veuillez me dire où il faut descendre.
vuh-yay muh DEER oo eel foh day-SAH<u>N</u>-druh

Customs / *La Douane*

385. Where is the customs?   Où est la douane?
oo eh la doo-AHNN

386. Here is my baggage, ___ pieces.
Voici mes bagages, ___ pièces.
vwah-SEE may bah-GAHZH, ___ pyehss

387. Here is my passport / visa.
Voici mon passeport / visa.
vwah-SEE maw<u>n</u> pass-PAWR / vee-ZAH

388. Must I open everything?   Dois-je tout ouvrir?
dwah-zhuh too too-VREER

389. I cannot open that.   Je ne peux pas l'ouvrir.
zhuh nuh puh pah loo-VREER

390. I have lost my key.   J'ai perdu ma clé.
zhay pehr-DEW mah KLAY

391. I have nothing to declare.   Je n'ai rien à déclarer.
zhuh nay ree-EH na day-kla-RAY

392. All this is for my personal use.
Tout ceci est pour mon usage personnel.
too suh-SEE eh poor maw new-ZAZH pehr-saw-NEHL

393. There is nothing here but ___.
Il n'y a rien que ___ ici.
eel nyah RYEHN kuh ___ ee-SEE

394. These are gifts. Ce sont des cadeaux.
suh sawn day kah-DOH

395. Are these things dutiable?
Ces choses sont-elles passibles des frais de douane?
say shohz sawn-tehl pa-SEE-bluh day freh duh doo-AHNN

396. How much must I pay? Combien dois-je payer?
kawn-BYEHN dwah-zhuh pay-YAY

397. This is all I have. C'est tout ce que j'ai.
seh TOO skuh ZHAY

398. Please be careful. Faites attention, s'il vous plaît.
feht za-tahn-SYAWN, seel voo pleh

399. Have you finished? Avez-vous fini?
ah-vay-voo fee-NEE

400. I cannot find my baggage.
Je ne peux pas trouver mes bagages.
zhuh nuh puh pah troo-vay may bah-GAHZH

401. My train leaves in ___ minutes.
Mon train part dans ___ minutes.
mawn TREHN par dahn ___ mee-NEWT

Tickets / *Les Billets*

402. How much is a ticket to ___?
Quel est le prix jusqu'à ___?
kehl eh luh pree zhew-skah

403. Where is the ticket office? Où est le guichet?
oo eh luh ghee-SHEH

404. One-way / round-trip ticket.
Un billet aller simple / aller-retour.
uhn bee-yeh AH-lay SEHN-pluh / AH-lay-ruh-TOOR

405. First / second class. Première / seconde classe.
PRUH-myehr / suh-GAWND klass

406. A reservation. A reserved seat.
Une réservation. Une place réservée.
ewn ray-zehr-vah-SYAWN, ewn plahss ray-zehr-VAY

407. Can I go by way of ___?
Puis-je y aller en passant par ___?
PWEE-zhuh ee ah-LAY ahn pa-SAHN par

408. How long is this ticket valid?
Jusqu'à quand ce billet est-il valable?
zhew-skah KAHN suh bee-yeh eh-teel vah-LAH-bluh

409. Must I stamp/validate the ticket?
Dois-je composter le billet?
dwah-zhuh kawn-paw-stay luh bee-YEH

TRAVEL AND TRANSPORTATION

Baggage / Les Bagages

410. Where is the baggage checked?
Où enregistre-t-on les bagages?
oo ahn-ruh-ZHEE-struh-tawn lay bah-GAHZH

411. I want to leave these bags for a while.
Je veux laisser ces valises un instant.
zhuh vuh leh-say say va-LEEZ uh nehn-STAHN

412. Do I pay now or later?
Dois-je payer maintenant ou plus tard?
dwah-zhuh pay-yay mehnt-NAHN oo plew TAHR

413. I want to take out my baggage.
Je veux retirer mes bagages.
zhuh vuh ruh-tee-RAY may bah-GAHZH

414. That is mine there.   Voilà la mienne.
vwah-LAH lah mee-EHNN

415. Handle this very carefully.
Faites attention avec celle-ci.
feht za-tahn-SYAWN ah-vehk sehl-SEE

Train / Le Train

416. Where is the train station?   Où est la gare?
oo eh lah GAR

417. I am going by train to ___.
Je prends le train pour ___.   *zhuh prahn luh trehn poor*

418. Is the train for ___ on time?
Est-ce que le train pour ___ est à l'heure?
ehs-kuh luh trehn poor ___ eh ta LUHR

The national railway companies of French-speaking countries include:

France	SNCF (Société nationale des chemins de fer français)
Belgium	SNCB (Société nationale des chemins de fer belge)
Switzerland	CFF (Chemins de fer fédéraux suisse)
Canada	Via Rail Canada

The local/regional trains include:

France	TER (transport express régional)
Belgium	Train L (Local)
Switzerland	Regio

Long-distance trains are typically called IC (InterCity / Intercités) in Europe and the two main high-speed trains include the TGV (train à grande vitesse) and Thalys which serve France, Belgium, Luxembourg, and Switzerland as well as other European countries bordering the Francophone areas.

Most European bus and train tickets must be validated after purchase by having a time stamp printed on them. These machines are usually on the platform for trains (make sure to validate your ticket BEFORE you get on the train!) or on the bus itself.

419. It is ___ minutes late.   Il a ___ minutes de retard.
eel ah ___ mee-NEWT duh ruh-TAR

420. At what platform is the train for ___?
À quel quai est le train pour ___?
ah kehl KAY eh luh trehn poor

421. Is this seat taken?
Est-ce que cette place est prise?
ehs-kuh seht plahss eh PREEZ

422. I have reserved this seat.
J'ai reservé cette place.
zhay ruh-zehr-vay seht PLAHSS

423. Please open (close) the window.
Voulez-vous bien ouvrir (fermer) la fenêtre.
voo-lay-voo byehn oo-VREER (fehr-MAY) la fuh-NEH-truh

424. Where is the dining car?
Où est le wagon-restaurant?
oo eh luh vah-GAWN-rehs-taw-RAHN

425. Does this train have Wi-Fi?
Est-ce qu'il y a une borne Wi-Fi dans ce train?
ehs-keel-yah ewn bawrn wee-fee dahn suh TREHN

Airplane / L'Avion

426. Is there a shuttle to the airport?
Y a-t-il une navette pour l'aéroport?
yah-teel ewn nah-VEHT poor la-ay-raw-PAWR

427. At what time will they come for me?
À quelle heure viendra-t-on me chercher?
ah keh luhr vyehn-drah-TAWN muh shehr-SHAY

428. When is there a plane to ___?
À quelle heure est le vol pour ___?
ah keh luhr eh luh vawl poor

429. Is food served on the plane?
Peut-on obtenir de quoi manger à bord?
puh-tawn awp-tuh-NEER duh KWAH mahn-ZHAY ah bawr

430. How long is the layover in Geneva?
La correspondance à Genève dure combien de temps?
lah kawr-uh-spawn-DAHNS ah zhuh-NEHV dewr kawn-byehn duh TAHN

431. How much baggage can I take?
Combien de kilos de bagages ai-je le droit d'emporter?
kawn-byehn duh kee-loh duh bah-GAHZH ay-zhuh luh drawh dahn-pawr-TAY

432. How much per kilogram for excess?
Combien par kilo pour l'excédent?
kawn-byehn par kee-LOH poor lehk-say-DAHN

433. Where is the check-in for my flight?
Où est l'enregistrement pour mon vol?
ooh eh lahn-reh-zhees-struh-MAHN poor mawn VAWL

434. Where do I check my bags?
Où est-ce je fais l'enregistrement de mes bagages?
OOH ehs-kuh zhuh feh lahn-reh-zhees-truh-MAHN duh may bah-GAHZH

43

435. I have jet lag. Je souffre de décalage horaire.
zhuh soof-ruh duh day-kah-LAHZH aw-REHR

436. Checked baggage. Carry-on bag.
Bagage de soute. Bagage à main.
bah-gahzh duh SOOT. bah-gahzh ah MEHN

437. Boarding card. La carte d'embarquement.
lah kahrt dawn-bar-kuh-MAHN

438. Departure gate. La porte d'embarquement.
la pawrt dawn-bar-kuh-MAHN

439. Departures. Arrivals. Départs. Arrivées.
day-PAHR. ah-ree-VAY

440. Entrance. Exit. Entrée. Sortie. *awn-TRAY.*
sawr-TEE

441. Delayed. Canceled. En retard. Annulé.
awn ruh-TAHR. ah-new-LAY

Bus / L'Autocar

442. A long-distance bus. Un autocar.
uh noh-taw-KAHR

443. Where is the bus station?
Où est la gare routière? *oo eh lah gar roo-TYEHR*

444. Where do I buy the ticket?
Où est-ce que j'achète le billet?
oo ehs-kuh zhah-SHEHT luh bee-YEH

445. Is there a stop for lunch?
Y a-t-il un arrêt pour le déjeuner?
ya-TEE-luh na-REH poor luh day-zhuh-NAY

Local Bus and Streetcar / L'Autobus et Le Tramway

446. A local bus. A streetcar.   Un autobus. Un tramway.
uh noh-taw-BEWSS. uhn trahm-WAY

447. Bus stop. The driver.   L'arrêt de bus. Le conducteur.
lar-reh de BEWSS. Luh kaw̲n-dewk-TUHR

448. What bus (tram) do I take to ___?
Quel bus (tram) dois-je prendre pour ___?
kehl bewss (trahm) dwah-zhuh prah̲n-druh poor

449. Where does the bus (tram) stop for ___?
Où s'arrête le bus (le tramway) pour ___?
oo sah-reht luh bewss (luh trahm-way) poor

450. Do you go near ___?   Passez-vous près de ___?
pah-say-voo preh duh

451. How much is the fare?   Combien?   *kaw̲n-BYEH̲N*

452. Must I validate the ticket?
Dois-je composter le billet?
dwah-zhuh kaw̲n-paw-stay luh bee-YEH

453. The next stop, please.
Le prochain arrêt, s'il vous plaît.
luh praw-sheh na-REH, seel voo pleh

Subway / Le Métro

454. Subway. Station.   Le métro. La station de métro.
luh may-TROH. lah sta-SYAW̲N duh may-TROH

455. Subway Line. Ticket.   La ligne de métro. Un ticket.
lah LEEN-yuh duh may-TROH. uhn tee-KAY

456. Booklet of 10 tickets.   Un carnet de tickets.
uhn kar-NAY duh tee-KAY

457. May I have a map of the subway?
Puis-je avoir un plan du métro?
PWEE-zhuh ah-vwahr uhn plawn dew may-TROH

458. What line should I take for ___?
Quelle ligne dois-je prendre pour ___?
kehl LEEN-yuh dwah-zhuh PRAWN-druh poor

459. Is this the stop for __?   C'est bien l'arrêt pour __?
seh byehn la-REH poor

Two Wheels and On Foot / Deux Roues et À Pied

460. I'd like to rent a bike / a scooter.
Je voudrais louer un vélo / un scooter.
zhuh voo-dreh loo-ay uhn vay-LOH / uhn SKOO-tehr

461. Do you have a helmet?   Avez-vous un casque?
ah-vey-voo uhn KAHSK

462. Are there bike paths?
Est-ce qu'il y a des pistes cyclables?
ehs-keel-yah day peest see-KLAH-bluh

463. Can I walk there?
Est-ce que je peux y aller à pied?
ehs-kuh zhuh puh ee ah-lay ah PYAY

464. It's fifteen minutes away.
C'est à quinze minutes d'ici.
seh tah kehnz mee-NEWT dee-SEE

465. Do you have a guide for local walks?
Avez-vous un guide des promenades?
ah-vay-voo uhn GHEED day prawm-NAHD

466. How long will the walk take?
Combien de temps dure la promenade?
kawn-byehn duh tahn dewr lah prawm-NAHD

467. It's two hours long. Elle dure deux heures.
ehl dewr duh ZUHR

Boat / Le Bateau

468. A river boat (for sightseeing).
Un bateau-mouche. *uhn BA-toh-MOOSH*

469. A ferry. Un ferry / Un traversier (Quebec).
uhn FEH-ree. / uhn trah-vehr-SYAY

470. A cruise. Une croisière. *ewn krwah-ZYEHR*

471. Can I go by boat to ___?
Puis-je aller par bateau à ___?
PWEE-zha-lay par ba-TOH ah

472. When does the next boat leave?
Quand le prochain bateau part-il?
kahn luh praw-shen ba-toh par-TEEL

473. When must I go on board?
Quand dois-je embarquer?
kahn dwah zhahn-bar-KAY

474. Can I land at ___? Pourrai-je débarquer à ___?
poor-RAY-zhuh day-bar-KAY ah

475. The port. The deck.   Le port. Le pont.
luh pawr. luh pawn

476. The captain. The steward.
Le capitaine. Le steward.
luh ka-pee-TEHNN. luh stew-AHR

477. I want to rent a deck chair.
Je voudrais bien louer une chaise longue.
zhuh voo-dreh byehn loo-ay ewn shehz LAWNG

478. I am seasick.   J'ai le mal de mer.
zhay luh mal duh MEHR

479. I am going to my cabin.   Je vais à ma cabine.
zhuh vay za ma ka-BEEN

480. Let's go to the dining room (to the bar).
Allons à la salle à manger (au bar).
a-LAWN zah lah sal ah mahn-ZHAY (zoh BAR)

481. A lifeboat.   Un canot de sauvetage.
uhn kah-noh duh sohv-TAHZH

482. A life preserver.   Une ceinture de sauvetage
ewn sehn-TEWR duh sohv-TAHZH

Taxi / Le Taxi

483. Please call a taxi for me.
Veuillez m'appeler un taxi.
vuh-yay mahp-LAY uhn tak-SEE

484. How far is it?   À quelle distance est-ce?
ah kehl dees-TAHNSS ehs

485. How much will it cost?   Quel sera le prix?
kehl suh-rah luh PREE

486. That is too much.   C'est trop cher.   *seh troh SHEHR*

487. What do you charge per hour (kilometer)?
Combien prenez-vous à l'heure (au kilomètre)?
kaw<u>n</u>-byeh<u>n</u> prun-ay-voo ah LUHR (oh
kee-law-MEH-truh)

488. I just wish to drive around.
Je veux simplement me promener en voiture.
zhuh vuh seh<u>n</u>-pluh-MAH<u>N</u> muh prawm-nay ah<u>n</u>
vwah-TEWR

489. Please drive more slowly (carefully).
Veuillez conduire plus lentement (prudemment).
vuh-yay kaw<u>n</u>-dweer plew lah<u>n</u>-tuh-MAH<u>N</u>
(prew-dah-MAH<u>N</u>)

490. Stop here. Wait for me.   Arrêtez ici. Attendez-moi.
ah-reh-TAY zee-see. at-TAH<u>N</u>-day-MWAH

491. How much do I owe?
Combien est-ce que je vous dois?
kaw<u>n</u>-BYEH<u>N</u> ehs-kuh zhuh voo DWAH

Car / La voiture

See the Appendix for more information on driving in Europe.

492. I would like to rent a car for one week.
Je voudrais louer une voiture pour une semaine.
zhuh voo-dreh loo-ay ewn vwah-TEWR poor ewn
suh-MEHNN

493. Do you have an automatic transmission car?

Avez-vous une voiture avec une boîte automatique?

*ah-vay-voo ewn vwah-TEWR ah-vehk ewn bwaht
aw-toh-mah-TEEK*

494. I can't drive a manual transmission.

Je ne conduis pas une boîte manuelle.

zhuh nuh kawn-dwee PAH ewn bwaht mah-NWEHL

495. Can I rent a GPS? Puis-je louer un système GPS?

PWEE-zhuh loo-ay uhn see-STEHM zhay-pay-EHS

496. I need a child seat. J'ai besoin d'un siège-bébé.

zhay buh-ZWEHN duhn syehzh-beh-BEH

497. Does the car have air conditioning?

Est-ce que la voiture a l'air conditionné?

ehs-kuh lah vwah-TEWR ah lehr kawn-dee-syaw-NAY

498. Does it have a large trunk?

Est-ce qu'elle a un grand coffre / une grande valise
(Quebec)? *ehs-kehl ah uhn grahn KAW-fruh / ewn
grahnd vah-LEEZ*

499. Does it take gas or diesel?

C'est une essence ou un diesel?

seh tew neh-SAHNSS oo uhn DYEH-zehl

500. Does this price include comprehensive insurance?

Est-ce que ce prix comprend l'assurance tous-risques?

*ehs-kuh suh PREE kawn-prahn lah-sew-rahns
too-REESK*

501. What is the fee to leave the car at another agency?
Quels sont les frais d'abandon pour laisser la
voiture dans une autre agence?
*kehl sawn leh freh dah-bahn-DAWN poor lehs-say
lah vwah-TEWR dahn zew-NOH-truh ah-ZHAHNS*

502. It's a rental car.   C'est une voiture de location.
seh-tewn vwah-TEWR duh loh-kah-SYAWN

503. Coupe (2 doors).   Un coupé.   *uhn koo-PAY.*

504. Sedan (4 doors).   Une berline   *ewn behr-LEEN*

505. Minivan.   Un monospace.   *uhn maw-naw-SPAHS.*

506. Station wagon.
Un break. / Une familiale (Quebec).
uhn brayk / ewn fah-meel-YAHL

507. A road map. A map of the city.
Une carte routière. Un plan de la ville.
ewn kahrt roo-TYEHR. uhn plahn duh lah VEEL

508. Where is there a gas station / garage?
Où y a-t-il une station service / un garage?
*oo yah-TEE lewn stah-SYAWN sehr-VEESS / uhn
gah-RAHZH*

509. Can you recommend a good mechanic?
Pouvez-vous m'indiquer un bon mécanicien?
*poo-vay-voo mehn-dee-KAY uhn bawn
may-kah-nee-SYEHN*

510. What town is this / the next one?
Comment s'appelle cette ville / la prochaine?
kawn-mahn sah-PEHL seht VEEL / lah praw-SHEHNN

511. Where does that road go?
Où cette route va-t-elle?   *oo seht root vah-TEHL*

512. Where is the entrance to the highway?
Où est l'entrée de l'autoroute?
oo eh lahn-TRAY duh law-toh-ROOT

513. Are there many rest areas?
Y a-t-il beaucoup d'aires de repos?
yah-TEEL boh-koo dehr duh ruh-POH

514. Are there tolls on the highway?
Y a-t-il des péages sur l'autoroute?
yah-TEEL day pay-AHZH sewr law-toh-ROOT

515. Do I have to buy a toll sticker?
Dois-je acheter une vignette?
dwahzh ahsh-TAY ewn veen-YEHT

516. I have an international driver's license.
J'ai un permis international.
zhay uhn pehr-MEE ehn-tehr-nah-syaw-NAHL

517. How much is gas / diesel per liter?
Combien coûte le litre d'essence / de diesel?
kawn-byehn koot luh LEE-truh deh-SAHNSS / duh DYEH-zehl

518. Give me ___ liters.   Donnez-moi ___ litres.
daw-nay-mwah ___ LEE-truh

519. Fill it up, please.   Le plein, s'il vous plaît.
luh PLEHN seel-voo-pleh

520. Please change the oil.   Veuillez changer l'huile.
vuh-yay shahn-zhay LWEEL

TRAVEL AND TRANSPORTATION

521. Recharge the battery.   Rechargez la batterie.
ruh-shar-ZHAY la bah-TREE

522. Tighten the brakes.   Resserrez les freins.
ruh-sehr-RAY lay FREH<u>N</u>

523. Will you check the tires?
Voulez-vous bien regarder les pneus?
voo-lay-voo byeh<u>n</u> ruh-gar-day lay PNUH

524. Can you fix the flat tire?
Pouvez-vous réparer le pneu crevé?
poo-vay-voo ray-pah-RAY luh pnuh kruh-VAY

525. A puncture. A slow leak.
Une crevaison. Une légère fuite.
ewn kruh-vay-ZAW<u>N</u>. ewn lay-zhehr FWEET

526. The _____ does not work well.
Le _____ ne marche pas bien.
luh _____ nuh marsh pah BYEH<u>N</u>

527. What is wrong? Qu'est-ce qu'il y a?   *kehs-keel-YAH*

528. My car has broken down.
Ma voiture est en panne.
mah vwah-TEWR eh taw<u>n</u> PAHNN

529. I cannot start the car.
Je n'arrive pas à démarrer la voiture.
zhuh nah-reev pah ah day-mah-ray lah vwah-TEWR

530. The battery is dead.   La batterie est à plat.
la baht-REE eh tah PLAH

531. It's out of gas.   Elle est en panne d'essence.
ehl eh taw<u>n</u> PAHNN deh-SAHNSS

532. There is a grinding / leak / noise.

Il y a un grincement / une fuite / un bruit.

eel yah uhn grehns-MAHN / ewn FWEET / uhn BRWEE

533. The engine overheats.

Le moteur devient trop chaud.

luh maw-TUHR duh-vyehn troh SHOH

534. The engine stalls.   Le moteur cale.

luh maw-tuhr KAHL

535. There is a rattle / squeak.

Il y a un cliquetis / un bruit aigu.

eel YAH uhn kleek-TEE / uhn brwee tay-GEW

536. My car is stuck in the mud / in the snow.

Ma voiture est embourbée / bloquée dans la neige.

mah vwah-TEWR eh tahn-boor-BAY / blaw-KAY dahn la NEHZH

537. It is in the ditch.   Elle est dans le fossé.

eh leh dahn luh faw-SAY

538. I am sorry to trouble you.

Je suis désolé(e) de vous déranger.

zhuh swee day-zo-LAY duh voo day-rahn-ZHAY

539. Can you help me jack up the car?

Pouvez-vous m'aider à lever la voiture avec le cric?

poo-vay-voo may-DAY ah luh-vay la vwah-TEWR ah-vehk luh KREEK

540. Will you help me put on the spare?

Pouvez-vous m'aider à mettre la roue de secours?

poo-vay-voo may-DAY ah MEH-truh la roo duh suh-KOOR

541. Could you give me some gas?
Pouvez-vous me donner de l'essence?
poo-vay-voo muh daw-nay duh leh-SAHNSS

542. Will you help me get the car off the road?
Voulez-vous m'aider à retirer la voiture de la route?
*voo-lay-voo may-DAY ah ruh-tee-ray lah vwah-TEWR
duh lah ROOT*

543. Can you tow me to the nearest garage?
Pouvez-vous me remorquer jusqu'au garage le plus
proche?
*poo-vay-voo muh ruh-mawr-KAY zhews-koh gah-
RAHZH luh plew PRAWSH*

544. Where is a parking lot? Où se trouve un parking?
oo suh troov uhn pahr-KEENG

545. May I park here for a while?
Puis-je me garer ici un peu?
PWEE-zhuh muh GAH-ray ee-SEE uhn puh

546. I want to park my car for the night.
Je veux garer la voiture pour la nuit.
zhuh vuh GAH-ray la vwah-TEWR poor la NWEE

547. When does it open / close?
À quelle heure est l'ouverture / la fermeture?
ah keh luhr eh loo-vehr-TEWR / la fehrm-TEWR

Parts of the Car / Les Parties de la Voiture

548. Accelerator. L'accélérateur. *lak-say-lay-rah-TUHR*

549. Battery. La batterie. *lah bah-TREE*

550. **Bolt.**   Le boulon.   *luh boo-LAWN*

551. **Break.**   Le frein.   *luh frehn*

552. **Engine.**   Le moteur.   *luh maw-TUHR*

553. **Nut.**   L'écrou.   *lay-KROO*

554. **Spring.**   Le ressort.   *luh ruh-SAWR*

555. **Starter.**   Le démarreur.   *luh day-mar-RUHR*

556. **Steering wheel.**   Le volant.   *luh vaw-LAHN*

557. **Headlight.**   Le phare.   *luh far*

558. **Tail light.**   Le feu arrière.   *luh fuh ar-RYEHR*

559. **Tube (of tire).**   La chambre à air.
lah SHAHN-brah EHR

560. **Tire.**   Le pneu.   *luh pnuh*

561. **Spare tire.**   Le pneu de secours.
luh pnuh duh suh-KOOR

562. **Wheel (front, back, left, right).**
La roue (avant, arrière, gauche, droite).
lah roo (ah-VAHN, ar-RYEHR, gohsh, drwaht)

Tools / *Les Outils*

563. **Chains**   Les chaînes   *lay shehnn*

564. **Hammer**   Le marteau   *luh mar-TOH*

565. **Jack**   Le cric   *luh kreekn*

566. **Key**   La clé   *lah klay*

567. **Pliers**   Les pinces   *lay pehnss*

568. **Rope** La corde *lah kawrd*

569. **Screwdriver** Le tourne-vis *luh toor-nuh-VEESS*

570. **Screw** La vis *lah veess*

571. **Tire pump** La pompe *lah pawnp*

572. **Wrench** La clé *lah klay*

573. **Drill** La perceuse *lah pehr-SUHZ*

574. **Jumper cables** Les câbles de démarrage
lay KAH-bluh duh day-mar-RAZH

ACCOMMODATIONS

Hotel / *L'Hôtel*

575. **Check-in time. Check-out time.**
L'heure limite d'arrivée. L'heure limite de départ.
luhr lee-MEET dah-ree-VAY. luhr lee-MEET duh day-PAHR

576. **Air conditioning.** La climatisation.
lah klee-mah-tee-zah-SYAWN

577. **High-speed Internet.** Internet à haut débit.
ehn-tehr-NEHT ah OH day-BEE

578. **Wireless Internet.** Le Wi-Fi. *luh wee-fee*

579. **Free. For a fee.** Gratuit. Payant.
grah-TWEE. peh-YAHN

Quick & to the Point: Hotel / L'Hôtel

Do you have any rooms available for tonight?
Avez-vous une chambre libre pour ce soir?
ah-vay voo ewn shahn-bruh lee-bruh poor suh SWAHR

I have a reservation for 3 nights.
J'ai une réservation pour trois nuits.
zhay ewn ray-zehr-vah-syawn poor trwah NWEE

How much is it per night?
Quel est le prix par nuit?
kehl eh luh pree pahr NWEE

What time is check-out?
À quelle heure faut-il libérer la chambre?
ah kehl uhr foh-teel lee-bay-ray lah SHAHN-bruh

Is breakfast included?
Est-ce que le petit déjeuner est compris?
ehs-kuh luh puh-tee day-zhuh-nay eh kawn-PREE

Are there any non-smoking rooms?
Y a-t-il des chambres non-fumeurs?
ee-ah-TEEL day shahn-bruh nawn-few-MUHR

Is the hotel handicap accessible?
L'hôtel est-il accessible aux personnes handicapées?
loh-TEHL eh-teel ahk-say-SEE-bluh oh pehr-sawn zahn-dee-kah-PAY

Do you accept animals?
Acceptez-vous les animaux?
ahk-sehp-tay-voo lay zah-nee-MOH

580. Which hotel is good / inexpensive?
Connaissez-vous un bon hôtel / à prix modéré?
kaw-neh-say-voo uh<u>n</u> baw noh-TEHL / ah pree
maw-day-RAY

581. The best hotel. Le meilleur hôtel.
luh may-YUH roh-TEHL

582. Not too expensive. Pas trop cher. pah troh shehr

583. I (do not) want to be in the center of town.
Je (ne) veux (pas) être au centre de la ville.
zhuh nuh vuh pah zeh-truh oh SAH<u>N</u>-truh duh lah VEEL

584. Where it is not noisy. Où il n'y a pas de bruit.
oo eel nyah pah duh BRWEE

585. I have a reservation for ___.
J'ai une réservation pour ___.
zhay ewn ray-zehr-va-SYAW<u>N</u> poor

586. I would like to reserve a room.
Je voudrais réserver une chambre.
zhuh voo-DREH ray-zehr-vay ewn SHAH<u>N</u>-bruh

587. I want a room with (without) meals.
Je désire une chambre avec (sans) repas.
zhuh day-zeer ewn SHAH<u>N</u> bra-vehk (SHAH<u>N</u>-bruh
sah<u>n</u>) ruh-PAH

588. Modified American plan. All inclusive.
Demi-pension. Tout inclus.
duh-mee pah<u>n</u>-SYAW<u>N</u>. too teh<u>n</u>-KLEW

589. I want a single / double room.
Je désire une chambre pour une personne / deux personnes. *zhuh day-zeer ewn SHAHN-bruh poor ewn pehr-SAWNN / duh pehr-SAWNN*

590. A room with a double bed.
Une chambre à grand lit pour deux. *ewn SHAHN brah grahn lee poor duh*

591. A suite. A bed. Un appartement. Un lit.
uh nap-par-tuh-MAHN. uhn lee

592. With bath / shower / twin beds.
Avec salle de bains / douche / lits jumeaux. *ah-vehk sahl duh BEHN / doosh / lee zhew-MOH*

593. With a window / a balcony.
Avec une fenêtre / un balcon. *ah-vehk ewn fuh-NEH-truh / uhn bal-KAWN*

594. Smoking. Non-smoking. Fumeur. Non-fumeur.
few-MUHR. NAWN-few-MUHR

595. For ___ days. For tonight.
Pour ___ jours. Pour cette nuit. *poor ___ ZHOOR. poor seht nwee*

596. For ___ persons. Pour ___ personnes.
poor ___ pehr-SAWNN

597. What is the rate for a day?
Quel est le prix par jour? *keh leh luh pree par ZHOOR*

598. Are tax and room service included?
Est-ce que les taxes et le service sont compris?
ehs-kuh lay TAX ay luh sehr-VEESS sawn kawn-PREE

599. Per week. Per month.   Par semaine. Par mois.
par suh-MEHNN. par MWAH

600. On what floor? À quel étage?
ah keh lay-TAHZH

601. Upstairs. Downstairs. En haut. En bas.
ahn OH. ahn BAH

602. Is there an elevator? Y a-t-il un ascenseur?
ya TEE luh nah-sahn-SUHR

603. I want a room higher up.
Je désire une chambre à un étage plus élevé.
zhuh day-zeer ewn SHAHN brah uh nay-TAHZH plew zay-luh-VAY

604. On a lower floor. Plus bas. *plew bah*

605. I would like to see the room.
Je voudrais bien voir la chambre.
zhuh voo-dreh byehn vwahr lah SHAHN-bruh

606. I (do not) like this one.
J'aime (je n'aime pas) celle-ci.
zhehm (zhuh nehm pah) sehl-SEE

607. Do you have something better?
Avez-vous quelque chose de meilleur?
ah-vay-voo kehl-kuh SHOHZ duh may-YUHR

608. Cheaper. Larger. Smaller.

Moins cher. Plus grand. Plus petit.

mweh<u>n</u> SHEHR. plew GRAH<u>N</u>. plew puh-TEE

609. With more light. More air.

Avec plus de lumière. Plus d'air.

ah-vehk plew duh lew-MYEHR. plew DEHR

610. Please call me at ___ o'clock.

Veuillez m'appeler à ___ heures.

vuh-yay map-PLAY ah ___ UHR

611. I want breakfast in my room.

Je voudrais prendre le petit déjeuner dans ma chambre.

zhuh vuh-dray PRAHN-druh luh peh-tee day-zhuh-NAY dah<u>n</u> ma SHAH<u>N</u>-bruh

612. Must I leave the key at the reception when I go out?

Dois-je laisser la clé à l'accueil quand je sors?

dwah-zhuh leh-say lah klay ah lah-KUH-yuh kah<u>n</u> zhuh SAWR

613. Could I have some laundry done?

Puis-je faire laver des affaires?

PWEE-zhuh fehr la-VAY day za-FEHR

614. I would like to speak to the manager.

Je voudrais bien parler au gérant.

zhuh voo-dreh byeh<u>n</u> par-lay oh zhay-RAH<u>N</u>

615. Do I have any letters or messages?

Y a-t-il des lettres ou des messages pour moi?

ya TEEL day LEH-truh oo day mehs-SAHZH poor mwah

616. I am leaving at ___ o'clock.   Je pars à ___ heures.
zhuh par ah ___ UHR

617. Please make out my bill.
Veuillez préparer ma note.
vuh-yay pray-pa-RAY mah NAWT

618. May I leave my baggage here until ___?
Puis-je laisser mes bagages ici jusqu'à ___?
PWEE-zhuh lehs-say may bah-GAHZH ee-SEE zhews-kah

619. Please forward my mail to ___.
Veuillez faire suivre mon courrier à ___.
vuh-yay fehr SWEE-vruh maw<u>n</u> KOOR-yay ah

Housekeeping / Le Ménage

620. Please open / close the windows.
Veuillez ouvrir / fermer les fenêtres.
vuh-yay zoov-REER / fehr-MAY lay fuh-NEH-truh

621. Do not disturb me until ___.
Ne me dérangez pas avant ___.
nuh muh day-rahn-zhay pah zah-VAH<u>N</u>

622. Please change the sheets today.
Veuillez changer les draps aujourd'hui.
vuh-yay shahn-zhay lay DRAH oh-zhoor-DWEE

623. Bring me another blanket / pillow.
Apportez-moi encore une couverture / un oreiller.
ah-pawr-tay-MWAH ahn-kawr ewn koo-vehr-TEWR / uh naw-ray-YAY

624. A pillow case. A bath mat.
Une taie d'oreiller. Un tapis de bain.
ewn TAY daw-ray-YAY. uhn ta-PEE duh behn

625. Hangers. A glass. The door.
Les cintres. Un verre. La porte.
lay SEHN-truh. uhn vehr. la pawrt

626. Soap. Towels. Le savon. Les serviettes.
luh sa-VAWN. lay sehr-VYEHT

627. Bathtub. Sink. La baignoire. Le lavabo.
lah behn-YWAHR. luh la-vah-BOH

628. Drinking water. Toilet paper.
L'eau potable. Le papier toilette.
loh paw-TAH-bluh. luh pap-YAY twah-LEHT

629. Is there always hot water?
Y a-t-il toujours de l'eau chaude?
ya-TEEL too-zhoor duh loh shohd

630. There is no hot water/toilet paper.
Il n'y a pas d'eau chaude / de papier toilette.
eel-nyah pah doh shohd / duh pap-YAY twah-LEHT

631. There are no bath towels.
Il n'y a pas de serviettes de bain / essuies de bain (Belgium).
eel-nyah pah duh sehr-VYEHT duh BEHN / eh-SWEE duh behn

632. The air conditioning doesn't work.
La climatisation ne fonctionne pas.
lah klee-ma-tee-zah-SYAWN nuh fawnk-syawnn PAH

633. The door handle is broken.
La poignée de porte / la clenche (Belgium) est cassée.
lah pwahn-YAY duh PAWRT / lah klehnsh eh kah-SAY

634. Can you empty the garbage?
Pouvez-vous vider les ordures / les vidanges (Quebec)?
*poo-vay-voo vee-day lay zawr-DEWR / lay
vee-DAHNZH*

635. Please come back later.   Veuillez revenir plus tard.
vuh-yay ruh-vuh-neer plew TAHR

Apartment / *L'Appartement*

636. I want a furnished apartment.
Je désire un appartement meublé.
zhuh day-zeer uh nap-par-tuh-MAHN muh-BLAY

637. Living room. Bedrooms.   Un salon. Des chambres.
uhn sah-LAWN. day SHAHN-bruh

638. Dining room. Kitchen.
Une salle à manger. Une cuisine.
ewn sal ah mahn-ZHAY. ewn kwee-ZEEN

639. (Fully equipped) kitchenette.
Une kitchenette (équipée).
ewn kee-cheh-NEHT (ay-kee-PAY)

640. Balcony. Bathroom.   Un balcon. Une salle de bains.
uhn bal-KAWN. ewn sal duh BEHN

641. Is the linen furnished?   Est-ce qu'on fournit le linge?
ehs-kawn foor-NEE luh LEHNZH

Key / La clé

Most European hotels require that you leave your room key at the front desk when you exit the building. If there is no 24-hour reception, then you will need to take it with you.

642. How much is it a week (a month)?
Quel est le loyer par semaine (par mois)?
keh leh luh lwah-yay par suh-MEHNN (par MWAH)

Household Items / Les Objets Ménagers

643. Ashtray. Un cendrier. *uhn SAHN-dree-ay*

644. Blankets. Les couvertures. *lay koo-vehr-TEWR*

645. Box. Une boîte. *ewn bwaht*

646. Broom. Un balai. *uhn bah-LEH*

647. Can opener. Un ouvre-boîte.
uh NOO-vruh-BWAHT

648. Candle. Une bougie. *ewn boo-ZHEE*

649. Clothes dryer.
Un sèche-linge. / Une sécheuse. (Quebec)
uhn SESH-lehnzh / ewn say-SHUHZ

650. Cork. Un bouchon. *uhn boo-SHAWN*

651. Corkscrew. Un tire-bouchon.
uhn TEER-boo-SHAWN

652. Curling iron. Un fer à friser. *uhn fehr ah free-ZAY*

653. Cushion. Un coussin. *uhn koo-SEHN*

654. Dish towel.
Un torchon. / Un essuie de cuisine (Belgium).
uhn tawr-SHAWN / uhn eh-swee duh kwee-ZEEN

655. Dishes. La vaisselle. *lah veh-SEHL*

656. Dishwasher soap. Un détergent pour lave-vaisselle.
uhn day-tehr-ZHAHN poor LAHV-veh-SEHL

657. Dishwasher. Un lave-vaisselle.
uhn LAHV-veh-SEHL

658. Dishwashing soap. Le liquide vaisselle.
luh lee-KEED veh-SEHL

659. Dustpan. Une pelle à poussière.
ewn pehl ah poo-SYEHR

660. DVD Player. Un lecteur de DVD.
uhn lek-TUHR duh day-vay-DAY

661. Electric burners. Les plaques électriques.
lay plahk zay-lehk-TREEK

662. Fabric softener. Un assouplissant textile.
uhn ah-soo-plee-SAHN tehk-STEEL

663. Flashlight. Une lampe de poche.
ewn lahmp duh pawsh

664. Flyswatter. Une tapette à mouches.
ewn tah-PEHT ah moosh

665. Garbage can. Une poubelle. *ewn poo-BEHL*

666. Glass. Un verre. *uhn vehr*

667. Hairdryer.
Un sèche-cheveux. / Un fœhn. *(Switzerland)*
uhn SEHSH-shuh-VUH / uh fuhn

668. Hook. Un crochet. *uhn kroh-SHAY*

669. Household cleaning products.
Les produits ménagers.
lay pro-DWEE may-nah-ZHAY

670. Iron. Un fer à repasser. *uhn fehr ah ruh-pah-SAY*

671. Ironing Board. Une planche à repasser.
ewn plahnsh ah ruh-pah-SAY

672. Kettle. La bouilloire. *lah boo-ee-WAHR*

673. Laundry detergent. Un détergent à lessive.
uhn day-tehr-ZHAHN ah leh-SEEV

674. Light bulb. Une ampoule. *ewn ahn-POOL*

675. Microwave. Un (four à) micro-ondes.
uhn (foor ah) mee-kroh-AWND

676. Padlock. Un cadenas. *uhn kahd-NAH*

677. Pail. Un seau. / Une chaudière *(Quebec)*
uhn soh / ewn shoh-DYEHR

678. Paper towel. L'essuie-tout. *leh-swee-TOO*

679. Plate. Une assiette. *ewn ah-SYEHT*

680. Radio. Une radio. *ewn RAH-dee-OH*

681. Refrigerator. Un réfrigérateur.
uhn ray-free-zhay-rah-TUHR

682. Scissors. Des ciseaux. *day see-ZOH*

683. Sheets. Les draps.   *lay drah*

684. Shovel. Une pelle.   *ewn pehl*

685. Silverware. Les couverts. / Les services. *(Switzerland)*
lay koo-VEHR / lay sehr-VEESS

686. Sofa. Un canapé.   *uhn kah-nah-PEH*

687. Sponge. Une éponge.   *ew nay-PAWNZH*

688. Telephone. Un téléphone.   *uhn tay-lay-FAWNN*

689. Television. Une télévision.
ewn tay-lay-vee-ZYAWN

690. Toaster. Un grille-pain.   *uhn GREE-yuh-PEHN*

691. Vacuum. Un aspirateur. / Une balayeuse *(Quebec).*
uh nah-spee-rah-TUHR / ewn bah-lah-YUHZ

692. Vase. Un vase.   *uhn vahz*

693. Washcloth.
Un gant de toilette. / Une débarbouillette *(Quebec).*
uhn gahn duh twah-LEHT / ewn DAY-bahr-boo-ee-YEHT

694. Washing machine.
Un lave-linge. / Une laveuse. *(Quebec)*
uhn lahv-LEHNZH / ewn lah-VUHZ

695. Window screen. Une moustiquaire.
ewn moo-stee-KEHR

696. Wire. Le fil.   *luh feel*

697. Wood. Le bois.   *luh bwah*

698. Workspace. Un espace bureau.
uh neh-SPAHSS bew-ROH

RESTAURANT AND FOOD

Restaurant / *Le Restaurant*

699. Where is there a good restaurant?

Où peut-on trouver un bon restaurant?

oo puh-tawn troo-vay uhn bawn rehs-taw-RAHN

700. Can you recommend an Italian restaurant?

Pouvez-vous recommander un restaurant italien?

*poo-vay-voo ruh-kaw-mahn-day uhn rehs-toh-RAHN
ee-tahl-YEHN*

701. I like Indian / Moroccan / Chinese cuisine.

J'aime bien la cuisine indienne / marocaine / chinoise.

*zhehm byehn lah kwee-ZEEN ehn-DYEHNN /
mah-roh-KEHNN / shee-NWAHZ*

702. Breakfast. Lunch. Dinner.

Le petit déjeuner. Le déjeuner. Le dîner. (France)

*luh puh-TEE day-zhuh-NAY. luh DAY-zhuh-NAY. luh
DEE-nay*

Le déjeuner. Le dîner. Le souper. (Quebec, Belgium,
Switzerland)

luh DAY-zhuh-NAY. luh DEE-nay. luh SOO-pay

703. A sandwich. A snack. Un sandwich. Un goûter.

uhn sahn-DWEETCH. uhn GOO-tay

704. A snack bar. A fast-food restaurant.

Une buvette. Un fast-food.

ewn bew-VEHT. uhn fahst-FOOHD

705. Dine in. Take-out. Manger sur place. À emporter.

mahn-ZHAY sewr plahss. ah awn-pawr-TAY

Quick & to the Point

Restaurant / *Le Restaurant*

What time do you open for dinner?
À quelle heure ouvrez-vous pour le dîner?
ah kehl uhr oo-vray-voo poor luh dee-NAY

Do you have menus in English?
Avez-vous des cartes en anglais?
ah-vay-voo day kahrt ahn ahn-GLEH

There are 4 of us.
On est quatre.
aw neh KAH-truh

We are ready to order.
On est prêt à commander.
aw neh PREH ah kaw-mahn-DAY

I would like . . .
Je voudrais . . .
zhuh voo-dreh

This is delicious.
C'est délicieux.
seh day-lee-syuh

The bill, please.
L'addition, s'il vous plaît.
lah-dee-SYAWN, seel voo pleh

Have a good meal.
Bon appétit.
baw nah-pay-tee

71

706. At what time is dinner served?

À quelle heure servez-vous le dîner?

ah keh luhr sehr-vay-voo luh dee-NAY

707. Can we have lunch (dinner) now?

Pouvons-nous déjeuner (dîner) maintenant?

poo-vawn-NOO day-zhuh-NAY (DEE-nay) mehnt-NAHN

708. The kitchen is closed. La cuisine est fermée.

lah kwee-ZEEN eh fehr-MAY

709. Waiter. Waitress. Head-waiter.

Le serveur. La serveuse. Le maître d'hôtel.

luh sehr-VUHR. lah sehr-VUHZ. luh MEH-truh doh-TEHL

710. Give me a table near the window.

Donnez-moi une table près de la fenêtre.

daw-nay-mwah ewn TAH-bluh preh duh la fuh-NEH-truh

711. At the side. In the corner. Sur le côté. Dans le coin.

sewr luh koh-TAY. dahn luh kwehn

712. Is this table reserved?

Est-ce que cette table est réservée?

ehs kuh seht TAH-bluh eh ray-zehr-VAY

713. We want to dine à la carte.

Nous voulons dîner à la carte.

noo voo-lawn dee-nay ah lah kahrt

714. Would you like a before-dinner drink?

Voulez-vous un apéritif?

voo-lay-voo uh nah-pay-ree-TEEF

715. Are you ready to order?
Êtes-vous prêt à commander?
eht-voo preh tah kaw-mahn-DAY

716. Menu. Fixed-price meal. Restricted fixed-price meal.
La carte. Le menu. Le formule.
lah kahrt. luh muh-NEW. luh fawr-MEWL

717. I want something simple / light.
Je veux quelque chose de simple / de légère.
zhuh vuh kehl-kuh SHOHZ duh SEHN-pluh / duh lay-ZHEHR

718. I like the meat rare / medium rare / medium / well done.
J'aime lah viande bleue / saignante / à point / bien cuite.
zhehm lah vee-ahnd bluh / sehn-YAHNT / ah PWEHN / byehn KWEET

719. I'm a vegetarian. Je suis végétarien / végétarienne.
zhuh swee vay-zhay-tah-RYEHN / vay-zhay-tah-ree-EHNN

720. I'm vegan. Je suis végétalien / végétalienne.
zhuh swee vay-zhay-tah-LYEHN / vay-zhay-tah-lee-EHNN

721. I'm allergic to peanuts / seafood.
Je suis allergique aux arachides / aux fruits de mer.
zhuh swee zah-lehr-ZHEEK oh zah-rah-SHEED / oh frwee duh MEHR

73

722. I'm lactose intolerant.

J'ai une intolérance au lactose.

zhay ewn eh<u>n</u>-taw-lay-RAH<u>N</u>S oh lahk-TOHZ

723. A plate. A glass. A napkin.

Une assiette. Un verre. Une serviette / une napkine (Quebec).

ew na-SYEHT. uh<u>n</u> vehr. ewn sehr-VYEHT / ewn nahp-KEEN

724. A knife. A fork. A spoon (large, small).

Un couteau. Une fourchette. Une cuillère (à soupe, à café).

uh<u>n</u> koo-TOH. ewn foor-SHEHT. ewn kwee-YEHR (ah SOOP, ah kah-FAY)

725. Bread. Butter. Cream.   Le pain. Le beurre. La crème.

luh peh<u>n</u>. luh buhr. la krehm

726. Sugar. Salt. Pepper.   Le sucre. Le sel. Le poivre.

luh SEW-kruh. luh sehl. luh PWAH-vruh

727. Sauce. Oil. Vinegar.   La sauce. L'huile. Le vinaigre.

la sohs. lweel. luh vee-NEH-gruh

728. This is not clean.   Ce n'est pas propre.

suh neh pah PRAW-pruh

729. A little more of this.   Un peu plus de ceci.

uh<u>n</u> puh plew duh suh-SEE

730. I'm full.   Je n'ai plus faim.   *zhuh nay plew FEH<u>N</u>*

731. I have eaten enough, thank you.

J'ai bien mangé, merci.

zhay byeh<u>n</u> mah<u>n</u>-ZHAY, mehr-SEE

732. This is overcooked. This is undercooked.
C'est trop cuit. Ce n'est pas assez cuit.
seh troh KWEE. suh neh pah za-say KWEE

733. This is too tough / sweet / sour.
C'est trop dur / sucré / amer.
seh troh DEWR / sew-KRAY / ah-MEHR

734. This is cold.   C'est froid.   *seh FRWAH*

735. I did not order this.   Je n'ai pas commandé cela.
zhuh nay pah kaw-mahn-day suh-LAH

736. May I change this for ___?
Pouvez-vous remplacer cela par ___?
poo-vay-voo rahn-pla-say suh-LAH par ___?

737. Do you need anything else?
Il vous faudra autre chose?
eel voo foh-DRAH oh-truh SHOHZ

738. How was it?   Ça a été?   *sah ah ay-TAY*

739. Cheers!   Santé!   *sahn-TAY*

740. Please pay at the cash register.
Veuillez payer à la caisse.
vuh-yay pay-yay ah la kehss

741. Is the tip included?   Le pourboire, est-il compris?
luh poor-BWAHR eh-TEEL kawn-PREE

742. Is the service charge included?
Le service, est-il compris?
luh sehr-VEES eh-TEEL kawn-PREE

743. Keep the change.   Gardez la monnaie.
GAHR-day lah maw-NAY

Hours and Bill / Les heures d'ouverture et l'addition

Many European restaurants close between 2:30 pm and 7 pm, which is useful to keep in mind when you arrive in a new city in the afternoon or evening. You most likely will not be able to eat a late lunch or early dinner. If a restaurant does remain open during the afternoon, the word *non-stop* will usually be on the door.

You MUST ask for the check at European restaurants. The server will never just bring it to you.

744. There is a mistake in the bill.
Il y a une erreur dans l'addition.
eel-ya ewn eh-RUHR dah__n__ lah-dee-SYAW__N__

745. What are these charges for?
Pourquoi ces suppléments?
poor-KWAH say sew-play-MAH__N__

Menu / Le Menu

This section has been alphabetized in French to facilitate the tourist's reading of French menus.

Appetizers / Les Hors d'œuvres

746. Potage. *poh-TAHZH.* **Soup.**

747. Salade verte. *sah-LAHD vehrt.* **Green salad.**

748. Soupe à l'oignon.   *soop ah lawn-YAWN.*   **Onion soup.**

749. Soupe au poulet.   *soop oh poo-LEH.*   **Chicken soup.**

750. Soupe aux légumes.   *soop oh lay-GEWM.* **Vegetable soup.**

Meat, Fish, and Seafood / La Viande, le Poisson, et les Fruits de Mer

751. Agneau.   *ahn-YOH.*   **Lamb.**

752. Bifteck.   *beef-TEHK.*   **Steak.**

753. Bœuf.   *buhf.*   **Beef.**

754. Canard.   *kah-NAR.*   **Duck.**

755. Crevettes.   *kruh-VEHT.*   **Shrimp.**

756. Dinde.   *dehnd.*   **Turkey.**

757. Foie.   *fwah.*   **Liver.**

758. Fruits de mer.   *frwee duh MEHR.*   **Seafood.**

759. Gigot.   *ZHEE-goh.*   **Lamb.**

760. Homard.   *aw-MAR.*   **Lobster.**

761. Huîtres.   *WEE-truh.*   **Oysters.**

762. Jambon.   *zhahn-BAWN.*   **Ham.**

763. Moules.   *mool.*   **Mussels.**

764. Oie.   *wah.*   **Goose.**

765. Poisson.   *pwah-SAWN.*   **Fish.**

766. Porc.   *pawr.*   **Pork.**

767. Poulet rôti. *poo-leh roh-TEE.* **Roast chicken.**

768. Poulet frit. *poo-leh FREE.* **Fried chicken.**

769. Rosbif. *raws-BEEF.* **Roast beef.**

770. Sardines. *sar-DEEN.* **Sardines.**

771. Saucisse. *saw-SEES.* **Sausage.**

772. Saucisson. *saw-see-SAW_N_.* **Salami.**

773. Saumon. *saw-MAW_N_.* **Salmon.**

774. Steak. *stehk.* **Steak.**

775. Steak haché. *stehk ah-SHAY.* **Ground beef.**

776. Une tranche de ___. *ewn trahnsh duh ___.*
A slice of ___.

777. Veau. *voh.* **Veal.**

Vegetables / Les Légumes

778. Asperges. *as-PEHRZH.* **Asparagus.**

779. Ail. *AH-yuh.* **Garlic.**

780. Carottes. *kah-RAWT.* **Carrots.**

781. Champignons. *shah_n_-peen-YAW_N_.* **Mushrooms.**

782. Chou. *shoo.* **Cabbage.**

783. Choucroute. *shoo-KROOT.* **Sauerkraut.**

784. Chou-fleur. *shoo-FLUHR.* **Cauliflower.**

785. Courgette. *koor-ZHEHT.* **Zucchini.**

786. Concombre. *kaw_n_-KAW_N_-bruh.* **Cucumber.**

787. Endive. *ahn-DEEV.* **Endive.**

788. Épinards. *ay-pee-NAHR.* **Spinach.**

789. Haricots. *ah-ree-KOH.* **Beans.**

790. Laitue. *leh-TEW.* **Lettuce.**

791. Maïs. *mah-EES.* **Corn.**

792. Oignon. *awn-YAW<u>N</u>.* **Onion.**

793. Persil. *pehr-SEEL.* **Parsley.**

794. Petits pois. *puh-tee PWAH.* **Peas.**

795. Piments. *pee-MAW<u>N</u>.* **Chili peppers.**

796. Poireau. *pwah-ROH.* **Leek.**

797. Poivrons. *pwahv-RAW<u>N</u>.* **Bell peppers.**

798. Pommes de terre (frites, bouillies).
pawm duh TEHR (freet, boo-YEE).
Potatoes (fried, boiled).

799. Purée de pommes de terre.
pew-RAY duh pawm duh TEHR. **Mashed potatoes.**

800. Tomates. *taw-MAHT.* **Tomatoes.**

Fruits and Nuts / *Les Fruits et les Noix*

801. Arachides. *ah-rah-SHEED.* **Peanuts** (Quebec).

802. Banane. *bah-NAHNN.* **Banana.**

803. Bleuet. *bluh-EH.* **Blueberry** (Quebec).

804. Cacahuètes. *kah-kah-WEHT.* **Peanuts** (Europe).

805. Cerises. *suh-REEZ.* **Cherries.**

806. Citron. *see-TRAW<u>N</u>.* **Lemon.**

RESTAURANT AND FOOD

807. **Citron vert.** *see-trawn VEHR.* **Lime.**

808. **Compote de pommes.** *kawn-POHT duh PAWM.* **Applesauce.**

809. **Fraises.** *frehz.* **Strawberries.**

810. **Framboises.** *frahn-BWAHZ.* **Raspberries.**

811. **Melon.** *muh-LAWN.* **Melon.**

812. **Melon d'eau.** *muh-lawn DOH.* **Watermelon** (*Quebec*).

813. **Myrtille.** *meer-TEE-yuh.* **Blueberry** (*Europe*).

814. **Noix.** *nwah.* **Walnuts.**

815. **Olives (noires, vertes).** *aw-LEEV (nwahr, vehrt).* **Olives (black, green).**

816. **Orange.** *aw-RAHNZH.* **Orange.**

817. **Pamplemousse.** *pahn-pluh-MOOS.* **Grapefruit.**

818. **Pastèque.** *pas-TEHK.* **Watermelon** (*Europe*).

819. **Pêche.** *pehsh.* **Peach.**

820. **Pomme.** *pawm.* **Apple.**

821. **Raisins.** *reh-ZEHN.* **Grapes.**

822. **Raisins secs.** *reh-zehn SEHK.* **Raisins.**

823. **Salade de fruits.** *sah-LAHD duh frwee.* **Fruit salad.**

Other Foods / D'Autre Nourriture

824. **Couscous.** *koos-koos.* **Couscous.**

825. **Frites.** *freet.* **Fries.**

826. **Fromage.** *froh-MAHZH.* **Cheese.**

827. **Nems.** *nehm.* **Egg rolls.**

828. **Nouilles.** *noo-EE-yuh.* **Noodles.**

829. **Pâtes.** *paht.* **Pasta.**

830. **Pizza.** *PEE-tsah.* **Pizza**

831. **Quiche.** *keesh.* **Quiche.**

832. **Riz.** *ree.* **Rice.**

833. **Taboulé.** *tah-boo-LAY.* **Taboule.**

Desserts / Les Desserts

834. **Brownie.** *brow-nee.* **Brownie.**

835. **Cake aux bananes.** *kehk oh bah-NAHNN.*
Banana bread.

836. **Cake aux courgettes.** *kehk oh koor-ZHEHT.*
Zucchini bread.

837. **Cake aux fruits.** *kehk oh FRWEE.* **Fruitcake.**

838. **Chocolat.** *shaw-kaw-LAH.* **Chocolate.**

839. **Confiture.** *kawn-fee-TEWR.* **Jam.**

840. **Cookie.** *KOOH-kee.* **Cookie.**

841. **Crème anglaise.** *krehm ahn-GLEHZ.*
Light custard cream.

842. **Crème dessert.** *krehm duh-SEHRT.* **Pudding.**

843. **Crêpe.** *krehp.* **Crepe / thin pancake.**

844. **Gâteau.** *gah-TOH.* **Cake.**

845. **Gaufre.** *GOH-fruh.* **Waffle.**

846. **Glace.** *glahss.* **Ice cream.**

847. **Mousse au chocolat.** *moos oh shaw-kaw-LAH.*
Chocolate mousse.

848. **Tarte.** *tahrt.* **Pie.**

849. **Tarte aux pommes.** *tahrt oh PAWM.* **Apple pie.**

850. **Tartelette.** *tahrt-LEHT.* **Tart.**

851. **Vanille.** *vah-NEE-yuh.* **Vanilla.**

852. **Yaourt.** *yah-OORT.* **Yogurt.**

Breakfast / *Le Petit Déjeuner*

853. **Pastries.** Viennoiseries / Couques (Belgium).
vee-ehn-nwahz-REE / koohk

854. **Croissant.** Croissant. *krwah-SAHN*

855. **Chocolate croissant.** Pain au chocolat.
pehn oh shaw-kaw-LAH

856. **Pastry with raisins.** Pain au raisin.
pehn oh reh-ZEHN

857. **Sweet bread.** Brioche. *bree-AWSH*

858. **Toast.** Pain grillé. *pehn gree-YAY*

859. **. . . with butter** . . . avec du beurre.
ah-vehk dew BUHR

860. **. . . with jam** . . . avec de la confiture.
ah-vehk duh lah kawn-fee-TEWR

861. . . . with honey   . . . avec du miel.
ah-vehk dew myehl

862. Cereal.   Des céréales.   *day say-ray-AHL*

863. Eggs (scrambled, fried).   Œufs (brouillés, au plat).
uh (broo-YAY, oh PLAH)

864. Eggs (soft-boiled, hard-boiled).
Œufs (à la coque, durs).
uh (ah la KAWK, dewr)

865. Omelet.   Omelette.   *awm-LETT*

866. Bacon.   Du bacon.   *dew bay-KUHN*

Beverages / Les Boissons

867. A drink. A cocktail.   Une boisson. Un cocktail.
ewn bwah-SAWN. uhn kawk-TEHL

868. Soft drink. Fruit drink.
Une boisson gazeuse. Un jus de fruit.
ewn bwah-sawn ga-ZUHZ. uhn zhew duh frwee

869. Beer (light, dark). Wine (red, white, rosé).
La bière (blonde, brune). Le vin (rouge, blanc, rosé).
*la byehr (blawnd, brewn). luh vehn (roozh, blahn,
roh-ZAY)*

870. Whiskey (with soda). Liqueur.
Le whisky (avec du soda). Une liqueur.
luh wees-KEE (ah-vehk dew saw-DAH). ewn lee-KUHR.

871. Cognac. Champagne.   Le cognac. Le champagne.
luh koh-NYAK. luh shahn-PAN-yuh.

872. Before-dinner drink. After-dinner drink.
Un apéritif. Un digestif.
uh nah-pay-ree-TEEF. uhn dee-zheh-STEEF.

873. A small (large) bottle of ___.
Une petite (grande) bouteille de ___.
ewn puh-teet (grahnd) boo-TAY duh

874. A glass of ___.   Un verre de ___.   *uhn vehr duh*

875. Beer.   Bière.   *byehr*

876. Draft beer.   Pression.   *preh-SYAWN*

877. Beer and lemonade.   Panaché.   *pah-nah-SHEH*

878. Cassis liqueur and white wine.   Kir.   *keer*

879. Espresso   Café   *kah-fay*

880. Double espresso   Grand café   *GRAHN kah-fay*

881. Coffee with cream   Café crème   *kah-fay krehm*

882. Coffee with milk   Café au lait   *kah-fay oh leh*

883. Coffee with a dash of milk   Café noisette
kah-fay nwah-zeht

884. Decaf coffee   Café déca   *kah-fay day-KAH*

885. Coffee with hot water   Café allongé
kah-fay ah-lawn-zhay

886. Hot chocolate   Chocolat chaud
shaw-kaw-lah shoh

887. Tea (plain)   Thé nature   *tay nah-tewr*

888. Tea with lemon   Thé au citron   *tay oh see-TRAWN*

889. Tea with mint   Thé à la menthe   *tay ah lah mahnt*

890. Herbal tea   Infusion / Tisane
ehn-few-syawn / tee-zahnn

891. Lemonade.   Citron pressé.   *see-TRAWN preh-SAY*

892. Lemon soda.   Limonade.   *lee-maw-NAHD*

893. Iced tea.   Ice tea / thé glacé (Quebec).
ice tea / tay glah-SAY

894. Lemonade with flavored syrup.   Diabolo.
dee-ah-boh-LOH

895. Syrup (to add to water).   Un sirop.   *uhn see-ROH*

896. Soda.   Un soda.   *uhn soh-DAH*

897. Diet soda.   Un soda de régime.
uhn soh-dah duh ray-JHEEM

898. Sparkling water.   Eau pétillante / gazeuse.
oh pay-tee-YAHNT / gah-ZUHZ

899. Still water.   Eau plate.   *oh plaht*

900. Pitcher of water.   Une carafe d'eau.
ewn kah-RAHF doh

901. Pitcher of wine.   Un pichet de vin.
uhn pee-sheh duh vehn

902. Half bottle.   Une demi-bouteille.
ewn DUH-mee boo-TAY

903. Ice cubes.   Des glaçons.   *day glah-SAWN*

Regional Specialties / *Les Spécialités Régionales*

904. Languedoc   **Cassoulet**
kah-soo-leh
Stew of meat (pork, beef, mutton)
and white beans

905. Provence   **Salade Niçoise / Ratatouille**
sah-lahd nee-SWAHZ / rah-tah-
TOO-wee
Mixed salad with tuna and anchovies / Stewed vegetable dish

906. Savoie   **Tartiflette / Raclette**
tahr-tee-fleht / rah-kleht
Potatoes, cheese and ham casserole / Potatoes & melted cheese

907. Lyon   **Quenelles**
keh-nell
Meat or fish dumplings

908. Burgundy   **Bœuf Bourguignon**
buhf boor-gheen-YAWN
Beef stew with onions and mushrooms

909. Bretagne   **Galette / Crêpe**
gah-leht / krehp
Flat, round cake / Thin, buckwheat
flour pancake

910. Lorraine   **Quiche Lorraine**
keesh law-rehnn
Egg and milk oven-baked dish

911. Belgium **Moules-Frites**
mool-FREET
Mussels and French fries

912. Switzerland **Fondue**
faw<u>n</u>-dew
Bread dipped in melted cheese

913. Quebec **Tourtière / Poutine**
toor-tyehr / poo-TEEN
Meat pie / French fries with cheese
curd and gravy

Regional Cheeses / Les Fromages Régionaux

914. Nord-Pas-de-Calais **Maroilles, Mimolette**
mahr-wahl, mee-maw-leht

915. Normandie **Camembert, Pont l'Evêque**
kah-mah<u>n</u>-behr, paw<u>n</u> leh-vehk

916. Lorraine **Munster**
muh<u>n</u>-STEHR

917. Ile-de-France **Brie de Meaux**
bree duh moh

918. Franche-Comté **Comté, Mont d'or**
kaw<u>n</u>-TAY, maw<u>n</u> DOHR

919. Savoie **Reblochon, Beaufort**
ruh-blaw-SHAW<u>N</u>, boh-fohr

920. Auvergne **Saint-Nectaire, Cantal**
seh<u>n</u>-nehk-tehr, kah<u>n</u>-tahl

921. Midi-Pyrénées	**Roquefort**
	rohk-fohr
922. Aquitaine	**Ossau-Iraty**
	aw-soh-ee-rah-tee
923. Switzerland	**Gruyère** grew-yehr

WHAT TO SEE

Sightseeing / *Faire du Tourisme*

924. Where is the tourist information office located?
Où se trouve l'office de tourisme?
oo suh troov law-FEES duh too-REES-muh

925. May I have a map of the city?
Puis-je avoir un plan de la ville?
PWEE-zhuh ah-VWAHR uhn plahn duh lah veel

926. What must we see in the city?
Que faut-il voir dans la ville?
kuh foh-teel vwahr dahn lah veel

927. Are guided tours available?
Est-ce qu'il y a des visites guidées?
ehs-keel-yah day vee-ZEET ghee-DAY

928. I would like a guide who speaks English.
Je désire un guide qui parle anglais.
zhuh day-ZEER uhn gheed kee par lahn-GLEH

929. Painting. Sculpture.   La peinture. La sculpture.
lah pehn-TEWR. lah skewl-TEWR.

Quick & to the Point

Sightseeing / Faire du Tourisme

castle	le château	luh sha-toh
cathedral	la cathédrale	lah ka-tay-drahl
church	l'église	lay-gleez
main square	la place	lah plahss
monastery	le monastère	luh maw-nah-stehr
monument	le monument	luh maw-new-mahn
mosque	la mosquée	lah maws-kay
museum	le musée	luh mew-zay
old city	la vieille ville	lah vyay veel
palace	le palais	luh pah-leh
ruins	les ruines	lay rew-een
statue	la statue	lah stah-tew
synagogue	la synagogue	lah see-na-gawg
temple	le temple	luh TAHN-pluh

930. **Beach. Garden. Botanical garden.**
   La plage. Le jardin. Le jardin botanique.
   *lah plahzh. luh zhahr-DEHN. luh zhahr-DEHN
   boh-tah-NEEK*

931. **Zoo. Playground. Amusement park.**
   Le zoo. L'aire de jeux. Le parc d'attractions.
   luh zoh. lehr duh zhuh. luh pahrk dah-trak-SYAWN

932. **What is the admission price?**
   Quel est le prix d'entrée?
   keh leh luh pree dahn-TRAY

933. **Where can I buy a ticket?**
   Où est-ce que je peux acheter un billet?
   OO ehs-kuh zhuh puh ahsh-TAY uhn bee-YAY

89

934. Is there a reduced price for students (children, seniors, groups)?

Est-ce qu'il y a un tarif pour étudiants (enfants, personnes âgées, groupes)?

ehs-keel-YAH uhn tah-REEF pour ay-tew-DYAHN (ahn-FAHN, pehr-sawnn zah-ZHAY, groop)

935. Where is the entrance (exit)?

Où est l'entrée (la sortie)?

oo eh lahn-TRAY (lah sawr-TEE)

936. What are the hours of operation?

Quelles sont les heures d'ouverture?

kehl sawn lay zuhr doo-vehr-TEWR

937. How much is an audio guide (a guidebook)?

Quel est le prix d'un guide audio (d'un guide)?

kehl eh luh pree duhn gheed oh-DYOH (duhn GHEED)

938. Is there a locker room (a coat room)?

Est-ce qu'il y a une consigne (un vestiaire)?

ess keel YAH ewn kawn-SEEN-yuh (uhn vehs-tee-EHR)

939. May I take photographs?

Est-il permis de prendre des photos?

eh teel pehr-MEE duh prahn-druh day faw-TOH

940. Do you sell postcards?

Vendez-vous des cartes postales?

vahn-day-voo day kahrt paws-TAHL

941. Can you take my (our) picture?

Pouvez-vous prendre une photo de moi (nous)?

poo-vay-voo prahn-druh ewn foh-toh duh mwah (noo)

Museums / Les musées

Many museums in Paris offer free admission on the first Sunday of the month. Some museums, such as Musée d'Orsay, Musée Rodin, and Musée du Quai Branly, are closed on Mondays. The Musée du Louvre and Centre Pompidou are both closed on Tuesdays.

Places of Worship / Les Lieux de Culte

942. A Catholic church. A Protestant church.
Une église catholique. Un temple protestant.
ew nay-GLEEZ ka-taw-LEEK. uhn TAHN-pluh praw-tehs-TAHN

943. A synagogue. A mosque. A Buddhist temple.
Une synagogue. Une mosquée. Un temple bouddhiste.
ewn see-na-GAWG. ewn maws-KAY. uhn TAHN-pluh boo-DEEST

944. Is there ___ nearby?
Y a-t-il ___ près d'ici?
ya TEEL ___ preh dee-SEE

945. May we go inside? Est-ce qu'on peut entrer?
ehs-kawn puh ahn-TRAY

946. Am I allowed to enter? Est-ce que j'ai le droit d'entrer?
ehs kuh zhay luh drwah dahn-TRAY

91

947. Must I cover my head? Dois-je couvrir ma tête?
DWAH-zhuh koov-reer mah teht

948. What time is mass (service)?
Quand est la messe (l'office)?
kahn teh la mehss (law-FEES)

949. Is there an English-speaking priest (pastor, rabbi, imam)?

·   Y a-t-il un prêtre (pasteur, rabbin, imam) qui parle anglais?
yah TEE luhn PREH-truh (pahs-TUHR, rah-BEHN, ee-MAHM) kee par lahn-GLEH

950. Where is there a service in English?
Où y a-t-il un office en anglais?
oo yah TEE luh naw-FEES ah nahn-GLEH

951. I am Christian / Protestant / Jewish / Muslim.
Je suis chrétien / protestant / juif / musulman. (masculine)
zhuh swee kray-TYEHN / praw-tehs-TAHN / zhweef / mew-suhl-MAHN
Je suis chrétienne / protestante / juive / musulmane. (feminine)
zhuh swee kray-TYEHNN / praw-tehs-TAHNT / zhweev / mew-suhl-MAHNN

952. Catholic. Buddhist. Atheist.
Catholique. Bouddhiste. Athée.
kah-toh-LEEK. boo-DEEST. ah-TAY

WHAT TO DO

Entertainment / *Le Divertissements*

953. Television. Movie theater.
La télévision. Le cinéma.
lah tay-lay-vee-ZYAWN. luh SEE-nay-MAH

954. News. Report. Program.
Les infos. Un reportage. Une émission.
lay zehn-FOH. uhn ruh-pawr-TAHZH. ew nay-mee-SYAWN

955. Series. TV movie.   Une série. Un téléfilm.
ewn SAY-ree. uhn tay-lay-FEELM

956. Reality TV. Game show.
La télé-réalité. Un jeu télévisé.
lah TAY-lay-ray-ah-lee-TAY. uhn zhuh tay-lay-vee-ZAY

957. Soap opera.
Un feuilleton. / Un téléroman. (Quebec)
uhn fuh-yee-TAWN / uhn tay-lay-raw-MAHN

958. Drama. Comedy.   Un drame. Une comédie.
uhn drahm. ewn KAW-may-dee

959. French version. Original (language) version.
Version française. Version originale.
*vehr-SYAWN frahn-SEHZ. vehr-SYAWN
oh-ree-zhee-NAHL*

960. Subtitled. Dubbed.   Sous-titré. Doublé.
soo-tee-TRAY. DOO-blay

Quick & to the Point

Types of movies / Genres de films

action	un film d'action	uhn feelm dak-syawn
adventure	un film d'aventure	uhn feelm dah-vahn-tewr
animated	un film d'animation	uhn feelm dah-nee-mah-syawn
independent	un film indépendant	uhn feelm ehn-day-pahn-DAHN
romantic comedy	une comédie romantique	ewn kaw-may-dee raw-mahn-TEEK
documentary	un documentaire	uhn daw-kew-mahn-tehr
science fiction	un film de science-fiction	uhn feelm duh see-ahnss-feek-syawn
fantasy	un film fantastique	uhn feelm fahn-tahs-teek
horror movie	un film d'horreur	uhn feelm daw-ruhr
western	un western	uhn wehs-tehrn
detective (film noir)	un polar	uhn poh-lahr
thriller	un thriller	uhn tree-luhr

961. Music. Concert. Opera.
La musique. Le concert. L'opéra.
Lah mew-ZEEK. luh kawn-SEHR. LOH-pay-RAH

962. Theater. Play. Le théâtre. La pièce de théâtre.
Luh tay-AH-truh. Lah pee-ESS duh tay-AH-truh

963. Is there a matinee today?
Y a-t-il matinée aujourd'hui?
yah teel mah-tee-NAY oh-zhoor-DWEE

964. What time does the show start?
À quelle heure commence le spectacle?
ah keh luhr kaw-MAHNS luh spehk-TAH-kluh

965. Is there an intermission? Y a-t-il un entr'acte?
yah tee luh nahn-TRAKT

966. Do you have any seats for tonight?
Avez-vous des places pour ce soir?
ah-vey-VOO day plahss poor suh SWAHR

967. An orchestra seat. A reserved seat.
Un fauteuil d'orchestre. Une place réservée.
uhn foh-TUH-yuh dawr-KEHS-truh. ewn plahss ray-zehr-VAY

968. In the balcony. The box. Au balcon. La loge.
oh bal-KAWN. la lawzh

969. Where can we go dancing?
Où pouvons-nous aller danser?
oo poo-vawn-noo ah-lay dahn-SAY

970. Do you want to dance? Voulez-vous danser?
voo-lay-VOO dahn-SAY

971. Cover charge. Minimum. Le couvert. Le minimum.
luh koo-VEHR. luh mee-nee-MUHM

972. Bar. Nightclub. Dance hall.
Un bar. Une boîte de nuit. Un dancing.
uhn bahr. ewn bwaht duh nwee. uhn dahn-SEENG

973. Bartender. Bouncer.   Le barman. Le videur.
luh bahr-MAHN. luh vee-DUHR

Sports and Activities / *Les Sports et les Activités*

974. I'm looking for a place nearby where I can ____.
Je cherche un endroit près d'ici où je peux ____.
zhuh shehrsh uh nahn-DRWAH preh dee-SEE oo zhuh puh

975. Play soccer.   Jouer au foot / au soccer (Quebec).
zhoo-AY oh FOOHT / oh saw-KEHR.

976. Play football.   Jouer au football américain.
zhoo-AY oh fooht-BOHL ah-may-ree-KEHN

977. Play rugby.   Jouer au rugby.
zhoo-AY oh ruhg-BEE

978. Play baseball.   Jouer au base-ball.
zhoo-AY oh behz-BOHL

979. Play basketball.   Jouer au basket.
zhoo-AY oh bah-SKEHT

980. Play volleyball.   Jouer au volley.
zhoo-AY oh vaw-LAY

981. Play tennis.   Jouer au tennis.
zhoo-AY oh teh-NEES

982. Play golf.   Jouer au golf.   *zhoo-AY oh gawlf*

983. Play hockey.   Jouer au hockey.
zhoo-AY oh aw-KEH

984. Play darts.   Jouer aux fléchettes.
zhoo-AY oh flay-SHEHT

985. Play pool.   Jouer au billard.
zhoo-AY oh bee-YAHR

986. Go bowling.   Jouer au bowling.
zhoo-AY oh BOO-leeng

987. Go ice skating.   Faire du patin à glace.
fehr dew pah-TEHN ah GLAHSS

988. Go skiing (downhill, cross-country).
Faire du ski (de piste, de fond).
fehr dew skee (duh peest, duh fawn)

989. Go snowshoeing.   Faire de la raquette.
fehr duh lah rah-KEHT

990. Go snowboarding.   Faire du snowboard.
fehr dew SNOH-bohrd

991. Go biking.   Faire du cyclisme.
fehr dew see-KLEES-muh

992. Go rollerskating.   Faire du patin à roulettes.
fehr dew pah-TEHN ah roo-LEHT

993. Go rollerblading.   Faire du roller.
fehr dew roh-LEHR

994. Go water skiing.   Faire du ski nautique.
fehr dew skee noh-TEEK

995. Go surfing.   Faire du surf.   *fehr dew suhrf*

996. Go wind-surfing.   Faire de la planche à voile.
fehr duh lah plahnsh ah vwahl

997. Go swimming.   Faire de la natation.
fehr duh lah nah-tah-SYAWN

998. Go sailing. Faire de la voile. *fehr duh lah vwahl*

999. Go boating. Faire du bateau. *fehr dew bah-TOH*

1000. Go hiking. Faire de la randonnée.
fehr duh lah rahn-daw-NAY

1001. Go climbing. Faire de l'escalade.
fehr duh lehs-kah-LAHD

1002. Go mountain climbing. Faire de l'alpinisme.
fehr duh lahl-pee-NEES-muh

1003. Go camping. Faire du camping.
fehr dew kahn-PEENG

1004. Where can I buy / rent ___?
Où est-ce je peux acheter / louer ___?
oo ehs-kuh zhuh puh ahsh-tay / loo-ay

1005. Skis. Des skis. *day skee*

1006. Ski shoes. Des chaussures de ski.
day shoh-SUHR duh skee

1007. Ski poles. Des bâtons de ski.
day bah-TAWN duh skee

1008. Snowshoes. Des raquettes. *day rah-KEHT*

1009. Skates. Des patins. *day pah-TEHN*

1010. Water skis. Des skis nautiques.
day skee noh-TEEK

1011. A sailboat. Un voilier. *uhn vwah-LYAY*

1012. A motor boat. Un bateau à moteur.
uhn bah-TOH ah maw-TUHR

1013. A paddle boat.   Un pédalo.   *uhn PAY-dah-LOH*

1014. A beach chair.   Un transat.   *uhn trahn-ZAHT*

1015. A beach umbrella.   Un parasol.
uhn pah-rah-SAWL

1016. A large ball (for soccer, football, basketball, etc.)
Un ballon.   *uhn bah-LAWN*

1017. A small ball (for tennis, golf, baseball, etc.)
Une balle.   *ewn bahl*

1018. A hockey puck.   Un palet. / Une rondelle (Quebec).
uhn pah-LEH. / ewn rawn-DEHL

1019. A tennis racket.   Une raquette de tennis.
ewn rah-KEHT duh teh-NEES

1020. A golf club.   Une crosse de golf.
ewn kraws duh gawlf

1021. Rollerblades.   Des rollers.   *day roh-LEHR*

Soccer / Le football

Les Bleus (the Blues) is the nickname of the French national soccer team, while the Belgian team is called Les Diables rouges (the Red Devils). The Swiss team goes by la Nati, which is short for national. Soccer, or more precisely football, is extremely popular in Europe and millions of fans tune into the Euro Cup and World Cup every 4 years as well as attend League games on a regular basis.

1022. A bike.   Un vélo.   *uhn VAY-loh.*

1023. A tent.   Une tente.   *ewn tahnt*

WHAT TO BUY

Shopping / *Le Shopping*

1024. I want to go shopping.
Je veux faire du shopping / magasiner. (Quebec)
zhuh vuh fehr dew SHAW-peeng / mah-gah-zee-NAY

Quick & to the Point

Shopping / Le Shopping

Do you have. . . ?
Avez-vous . . . ?
ah-vay voo

How much?
Combien?
kawn-byehn

This one / That one
Celui-ci / Celui-là
suh-lwee-see / suh-lwee-lah

That's too expensive.
C'est trop cher.
seh troh shehr

It's too big / Too small.
C'est trop grand / petit.
seh troh grahn / puh-tee

It's too long / short.
C'est trop long / court.
seh troh lawn / koor

I don't like it.
Je n'aime pas.
zhuh nehm pah

I'm just looking.
Je regarde seulement.
zhuh ruh-gahrd suhl-mahn

I'll think it over.
Je vais réfléchir.
zhuh veh ray-flay-sheer

1025. I want to buy ___. Je veux acheter ___.
zhuh vuh zahsh-TAY

1026. I prefer something cheaper.
Je préfère quelque chose de moins cher.
zhuh pray-FEHR kehl-kuh-SHOHZ duh mwehn shehr

1027. May I try this on? Puis-je l'essayer?
PWEE-zhuh lehs-say-YAY

1028. It does not fit me. Il ne me va pas.
eel nuh muh vah pah

1029. I need a larger (smaller) size.
J'ai besoin d'une taille plus grande (plus petite).
zhay buh-ZWEHN dewn TY-uh plew grahnd (plew
puh-TEET)

1030. I'd like to pay with cash / credit card.
Je voudrais payer en espèces / avec ma carte de
crédit.
zhuh vood-REH pay-YAY ahn eh-SPESS / ah-vehk mah
kahrt duh kray-DEE

1031. May I order one (online)?
Puis-je en commander un (sur Internet)?
PWEE-zhuh ahn kaw-mahn-day uhn (sewr
ehn-tehr-NEHT)

1032. How long will it take?
Combien de temps dois-je attendre?
kawn-BYEHN duh tahn dwah-zhuh ah-TAHN-druh

1033. Do you ship internationally?
Est-ce que vous expédiez à l'étranger?
ehs-kuh voo zeks-pay-dee-AY ah lay-trahn-ZHAY

WHAT TO BUY

1034. Receipt.   Un ticket de caisse.   *uhn tee-keh duh kess.*

1035. Bag.

Un sac. / Un cornet. (Eastern France and Switzerland)
uhn sahk / uhn kawr-NEH

1036. No returns, exchanges, or refunds.

Ni repris, ni échangés, ni remboursés.
nee ruh-PREE, nee ay-shahn-ZHAY, nee rahn-boor-SAY

Stores / Les Magasins

1037. Where is a clothing store?

Où est un magasin de vêtements?
oo eh tuhn mah-gah-ZEHN duh veht-MAHN

1038. Shoe store.   Un magasin de chaussures.
uhn mah-gah-ZEHN duh shoh-SUHR

1039. Department store.   Un grand magasin.
uhn grahn mah-gah-ZEHN

1040. Jewelry store.   Une bijouterie.   *ewn bee-zhoo-TREE*

1041. Electronics store.   Un magasin d'électronique.
uhn mah-gah-ZEHN day-lehk-traw-NEEK

1042. Bookstore.   Un librairie.   *uhn lee-breh-REE*

1043. Stationery store.   Une papeterie.   *ewn pah-pay-TREE*

1044. Souvenir shop.   Un magasin de souvenirs.
uhn mah-gah-ZEHN duh soov-NEER

1045. Newsstand.   Un kiosque.   *uhn KEE-awsk*

1046. Tobacconist's.   Un tabac.   *uhn TAH-bah*

1047. Flower shop.   Un fleuriste.   *uhn fluhr-EEST*

1048. Bakery. Une boulangerie. *ewn boo-lahnzh-REE*

1049. Pastry shop. Une pâtisserie. *ewn pah-tees-REE*

1050. Candy store. Une confiserie. *ewn kaw<u>n</u>-fees-REE*

1051. Butcher. Un boucher. *uh<u>n</u> BOO-shay*

1052. Fish merchant. Un poissonnerie.
uh<u>n</u> pwah-sawnn-REE

1053. Supermarket. Un supermarché.
uh<u>n</u> soo-pehr-mahr-SHAY

Stores / Les magasins

Remember to always say "bonjour" or "bonsoir" when entering a store. In Europe, many shops are closed between 12 and 2 pm and the closing times are generally around 7 pm for smaller boutiques and 9 pm for larger supermarkets. Very few stores are open on Sundays, with some exceptions in the major tourist areas. Sales are generally only allowed twice a year in January and July in France and Belgium, though government regulations have been easing up on this in recent years.

You will need to convert American sizes to European sizes for clothing. For women, add 32 to the American size to get the French size and add 30 to get the Belgian or Swiss size. Men's clothing tends to use centimeters instead of inches, so simply multiply the U.S. size by 2.54. For shoes, add 32.

103

1054. **Superstore.**   Un hypermarché.
uhn EE-pehr-mahr-SHAY

1055. **Open-air market.**   Un marché en plein air.
uhn mahr-SHAY ahn pleh-NEHR

1056. **Flea market.**   Un marché aux puces.
uhn mahr-SHAY oh pewss

1057. **Grocery or convenience store.**
Une épicerie. / Un dépanneur (Quebec).
ewn AY-pees-REE / uhn DAY-pahn-NUHR

Quantities and Measurements / *Les Quantités et les Dimensions*

1058. **A little bit of ___.**   Un petit peu de ___.
uhn puh-TEE puh duh

1059. **A handful of ___.**   Une poignée de ___.
ewn pwah-NYAY duh

1060. **A (half-)kilo of ___.**   Un (demi-)kilo de ___.
uhn (DUH-mee)kee-LOH duh

1061. **A (half-)bottle of ___.**
Une (demi-)bouteille de ___.
ewn (DUH-mee)boo-TAY duh

1062. **A glass of ___.**   Un verre de ___.
uhn vehr duh

1063. **A liter of ___.**   Un litre de ___.   *uhn LEET-ruh duh*

1064. **A piece of ___.**   Un morceau de ___.
uhn mohr-SOH duh

1065. A slice of ___.   Une tranche de ___.
ewn trahnsh duh

1066. A package/box/can of ___.   Une boîte de ___.
ewn bwaht duh

1067. A jar of ___.   Un pot de ___.   *uhn poh duh*

1068. That's enough.   C'est assez.   *seh tah-SAY*

1069. A pair. A dozen.   Une paire. Une douzaine.
ewn pehr. ewn doo-ZEHNN

1070. Half a dozen.   Une demi-douzaine.
ewn DUH-mee-doo-ZEHNN

1071. Half a meter.   Cinquante centimètres.
sehn-KAHNT sahn-tee-MEH-truh

1072. What is the length (width)?
Quelle est la longueur (largeur)?
keh leh lah lawn-GUHR (lar-ZHUHR)

1073. How much is it per meter?   Combien le mètre?
kawn-BYEHN luh MEH-truh

1074. What is the size?   Quelle est la taille?
keh leh lah TY-uh
Quelle est la pointure? (shoes)
keh leh lah pwehn-TEWR

1075. It is ten meters long by four meters wide.
Il a dix mètres de long sur quatre mètres de large.
ee-lah dee MEH-truh duh lawn sewr KAH-truh MEH-truh duh lahrzh

1076. High. Low.   Haut. Bas.   *oh. bah*

1077. Large. Small. Medium.
Grand. Petit. Moyen. (masculine)
grahn. puh-TEE. mwah-YEHN
Grande. Petite. Moyenne. (feminine)
grahnd. puh-TEET. mwah-YEHNN

1078. Alike. Different. Semblable. Différent / Différente.
sahn-BLAH-bluh. dee-fay-RAHN / dee-fay-RAHNT

Colors and Patterns / Les Couleurs et les Motifs

1079. Black. Noir / Noire. *nwahr*

1080. Blue. Bleu / Bleue. *bluh*

1081. Brown. Brun / Brune. *bruhn / brewn*

1082. Chestnut brown. Marron. *mah-rawn*

1083. Golden. Doré / Dorée. *doh-RAY*

1084. Gray. Gris / Grise. *gree / greez*

1085. Green. Vert / Verte. *vehr / vehrt*

1086. Orange. Orange. *or-AHNZH*

1087. Pink. Rose. *rohz*

1088. Purple. Violet / Violette. *vee-oh-LAY / vee-oh-LEHT*

1089. Red. Rouge. *roozh*

1090. Silver. Argenté / Argentée. *ahr-zhahn-TAY*

1091. White. Blanc / Blanche. *blahn / blahnsh*

1092. Yellow. Jaune. *zhohn*

1093. Light. Clair / Claire. *klehr*

1094. Dark. Foncé / Foncée. *fawn-SAY*

1095. Striped. À rayures. *ah ray-EWR*

1096. Plaid. À carreaux. *ah kah-ROH*

1097. Dotted. À pois. *ah pwah*

1098. Flowery. À fleurs. *ah fluhr*

1099. Frilly. À froufrous. *ah froo-froo*

Souvenir Shop / Magasin de Souvenirs

1100. Postcard. Une carte postale.
ewn kahrt paw-STAHL

1101. Calendar. Un calendrier. *uhn kah-lahn-dree-YAY*

1102. Magnet. Un magnet. *uhn mahn-YET*

1103. Mug. Une grande tasse. / Un mug.
ewn grahnd tahs / uhn muhg

1104. Beer mug/stein. Une chope à bière.
ewn shawp ah BYEHR

1105. Shot glass. Un verre à shooter.
uhn vehr-ah-shoo-TEHR

1106. Bell. Une clochette. *ewn klaw-SHEHT*

1107. Spoon. Une cuillère. *ewn kwee-YEHR*

1108. Key ring. Un porte-clés. *uhn pawrt-KLAY*

1109. Candy. Des bonbons. *day bawn-BAWN*

1110. Chewing gum. Du chewing-gum.
dew chew-eeng-GUHM

1111. Apron. Un tablier. *uhn tah-blee-AY*

1112. Coaster. Un sous-verre. *uhn SOO-vehr*

1113. Oven mitt. Une manique. *ewn mah-NEEK*

1114. Kitchen towel. Un torchon. *uhn tawr-SHAWN*

1115. Pen. Un stylo. *uhn stee-LOH*

1116. Lighter. Un briquet. *uhn bree-KAY*

1117. T-shirt. Un t-shirt. *uhn TEE-shirt*

1118. Cap. Un casquette. *uhn kahs-KEHT*

1119. Doll. Une poupée. *ewn poo-PAY*

1120. Knickknack. Un bibelot. *uhn BEEB-loh*

1121. Stuffed animal. Un animal en peluche.
uh nah-nee-MAHL ahn puh-LEWSH

1122. Puzzle. Un puzzle. *uhn PUH-zuhl*

1123. Snow globe. Une boule de neige.
ewn bool duh nehzh

1124. Picture frame. Un cadre photo.
uhn kahd-ruh foh-TOH

1125. Clock. Un horloge. *uh nawr-LAWZH*

1126. Flag. Un drapeau. *uhn drah-POH*

1127. Bookmark. Un marque-page. *uhn mahrk-PAHZH*

1128. Letter opener. Un coupe-papier.
uhn KOOP-pah-PYAY

1129. Pencil case. Une trousse. *ewn trooss*

1130. Pencil sharpener. Un taille-crayon.
uhn ty-uh-kreh-YAWN

1131. Mousepad. Un tapis de souris.
uhn tah-PEE duh soo-REE

Clothing and Accessories / Les Vêtements et les Accessoires

Clothing / Les Vêtements

1132. Belt. Une ceinture. *ewn seh<u>n</u>-TEWR*

1133. Blouse. Un chemisier. *uh<u>n</u> shmee-ZYAY*

1134. Boxers. Un caleçon. *uh<u>n</u> kahl-SAW<u>N</u>*

1135. Briefs. Un slip. *uh<u>n</u> sleep*

1136. Bra. Un soutien-gorge. *uh<u>n</u> SOO-tyeh<u>n</u>-GAWRZH*

1137. Cap (baseball). Un casquette. *uh<u>n</u> kahs-KEHT*

1138. Cardigan. Un gilet. *uh<u>n</u> ZHEE-lay*

1139. Clothes. Les vêtements. / Les hardes (*Acadia*). *lay veht-MAH<u>N</u> / lay ahrd*

1140. Coat. Un manteau. *uh<u>n</u> mah<u>n</u>-TOH*

1141. Collar. Un col. *uh<u>n</u> kohl*

1142. Decorative scarf. Un foulard. *uh<u>n</u> FOO-lahr*

1143. Dress. Une robe. *ewn rohb*

1144. Glasses. Les lunettes. *lay lew-NEHT*

1145. Gloves. Les gants. *lay gah<u>n</u>*

1146. Handbag. Un sac à main. *uh<u>n</u> sahk-ah-MEH<u>N</u>*

1147. Handkerchief. Un mouchoir. *uh<u>n</u> moosh-WAHR*

1148. Hat (standard). Un chapeau. *uh<u>n</u> shah-POH*

1149. Hat (wool/knit). Un bonnet. / Une tuque (*Quebec*). *uh<u>n</u> baw-NAY / ewn tewk*

1150. Jacket. Une veste. *ewn vehst*

1151. Jacket (leather). Une veste en cuir.
ewn vehs tahn KWEER

1152. Jeans. Un jean. *uhn zheen*

1153. Jersey (sports).
Un maillot. / Un chandail de joueur (*Quebec*).
uhn MY-oh / uhn shahn-dy duh zhoo-UHR

1154. Mitten. Une moufle. *ewn MOOF-luh*

1155. Necktie. Une cravate. *ewn krah-VAHT*

1156. Nightgown. Une chemise de nuit.
ewn shuh-meez duh nwee

1157. Outfit. Un ensemble. *uhn ahn-SAHN-bluh*

1158. Pajamas. Un pyjama. *uhn PEE-zhah-mah*

1159. Panties. Des culottes. *day kew-LAWT*

1160. Pants (pair of). Un pantalons. *uhn pahn-tah-LAWN*

1161. Polo shirt. Un polo. *uhn POH-loh*

1162. Purse (for change). Un porte-monnaie.
uhn pawrt-maw-NAY

1163. Purse. Un sac à main. *uhn sahk ah MEHN*

1164. Raincoat. Un imperméable.
uh nehn-pehr-may-AH-bluh

1165. Robe. Un peignoir. *uhn pehn-WAHR*

1166. Scarf. Une écharpe. *ew nay-SHARP*

1167. Shirt. Une chemise. *ewn shuh-MEEZ*

1168. Shorts. Un short. *uhn shohrt*

1169. Skirt. Une jupe. *ewn zhewp*

1170. Sleeve. Une manche. *ewn mah<u>n</u>sh*

1171. Slip. Une jupette. *ewn zhew-PEHT*

1172. Sunglasses. Des lunettes de soleil.
day lew-NEHT duh soh-LAY

1173. Suit (men). Un costume. *uh<u>n</u> kaw-stewm.*

1174. Suit (women). Un tailleur. *uh<u>n</u> ty-UHR*

1175. Suspenders. Les bretelles. *lay bruh-TEHL*

1176. Sweater. Un pull. / Un chandail (Quebec).
uh<u>n</u> pewl / uh<u>n</u> shah<u>n</u>-dy

1177. Swimsuit. Un maillot de bain. *uh<u>n</u> MY-oh duh BEH<u>N</u>*

1178. Tank top. Un débardeur. *uh<u>n</u> DAY-bahr-DUHR*

1179. Trenchcoat. Un trench. *uh<u>n</u> treh<u>n</u>sh*

1180. Underwear. Des sous-vêtements.
day SOO-veht-MAH<u>N</u>

1181. Umbrella. Un parapluie. *uh<u>n</u> pah-rah-plew-EE*

1182. Vest. Un gilet. *uh<u>n</u> ZHEE-lay*

1183. Wallet. Un portefeuille. *uh<u>n</u> pawr-tuh-FUH-yee*

Footwear / Les Chaussures

1184. Boots. Des bottes. *day bawt*

1185. Flats (ballerina shoes). Des ballerines.
day bahl-uh-REEN

1186. Flip-flops. Des tongs. *day taw<u>n</u>g*

1187. High heels. Des talons hauts. / Des escarpins.
day tah-LAW<u>N</u> oh / day ZEHS-kahr-PEH<u>N</u>

1188. Sandals. Des sandales. *day sah<u>n</u>-DAHL*

1189. Shoe. Une chaussure. / Un soulier.
ewn shoh-SUHR / uh<u>n</u> sool-YAY

1190. Slipper. Une pantoufle. / Un chausson.
ewn pah<u>n</u>-TOOF-luh / uh<u>n</u> shoh-SAW<u>N</u>

1191. Sneakers. Des baskets. *day bah-SKEHT*

1192. Socks. Des chausettes. *day shoh-SEHT*

1193. Stockings. Des bas. *day bah*

Jewelry / Les Bijoux

1194. Bracelet. Un bracelet. *uh<u>n</u> brahs-LAY*

1195. Jewelry. Les bijoux. *lay BEE-zhoo*

1196. Necklace. Un collier. *uh<u>n</u> kawl-YAY*

1197. Ring. Une bague / Un anneau.
ewn bahg / uh nah-NOH

1198. Earrings. Des boucles d'oreilles.
day BOOK-luh doh-RAY

1199. Watch. Une montre. *ewn MAW<u>N</u>-truh*

1200. Gold. L'or. *lohr*

1201. Silver. L'argent. *lahr-zhah<u>n</u>*

Fabrics / *Les Étoffes*

1202. Cotton. Le coton. *luh koh-TAWN*

1203. Silk. La soie. *lah swah*

1204. Linen. Le lin. *luh lehn*

1205. Wool. La laine. *lah lehnn*

Notions / *Les Accessoires*

1206. Bobby pins. Des épingles à cheveux.
day zay-PEHN-gluh ah shuh-VUH

1207. Shoelace. Un lacet. *uhn lah-SEH*

1208. Strap. Une bretelle. *ewn bruh-TEHL*

1209. Button. Un bouton. *uhn BOO-tawn*

1210. Needle. Une aiguille. *ew neh-GWEE*

1211. Thread. Le fil. *luh feel*

1212. Thimble. Un dé à coudre. *uhn day ah KOO-druh*

1213. Pin. Une épingle. *ew nay-PEHN-gluh*

1214. Safety pin. Une épingle de sûreté.
ew nay-pehn-gluh duh sewr-TAY

1215. Zipper. Une fermeture éclair. / Une tirette (*Belgium*).
ewn fehr-muh-TEWR ay-KLEHR / ewn TEE-reht

Photography / *La Photographie*

1216. Disposable camera. Un appareil photo jetable.
uh nah-pah-RAY foh-TOH zhuh-TAH-bluh

1217. Digital camera. Un appareil photo numérique.
uh nah-pah-RAY foh-TOH new-may-REEK

1218. Memory card. Une carte mémoire.
ewn kahrt MAYM-wahr

1219. The memory card is full.
La carte mémoire est pleine.
lah kahrt MAYM-wahr eh PLEHNN

1220. The battery is dead. La batterie est morte.
la baht-REE eh mawrt

1221. I need to recharge the battery.
J'ai besoin de recharger la batterie.
zhay buh-ZWEHN duh ruh-shahr-ZHAY la baht-REE

1222. Where can I find an adapter?
Où est-ce que je peux trouver un adaptateur?
oo eh-skuh zhuh puh troo-VAY uh nah-dahp-tah-TUHR

1223. Do you have film (batteries) for this camera?
Avez-vous une pellicule (des piles) pour cet appareil
photo?
*ah-vay-voo ewn pehl-ee-KEWL (day peel) poor seht
ah-pah-RAY foh-TOH*

1224. What types of lenses do you carry?
Qu'est-ce que vous avez comme objectifs?
kehs-kuh voo-zah-VAY kawm awb-zhehk-TEEF

1225. Do you sell cleaning kits?
Vendez-vous des kits de nettoyage?
vahn-day-voo day keet duh neh-twah-YAHZH

Bookstore and Newsstand / *La Librairie et le Kiosque*

1226. I'm looking for a phrase book.
Je cherche un manuel de conversation.
zhuh shehrsh uhn mah-new-EHL duh kawn-vehr-sah-SYAWN

1227. Dictionary.   Un dictionnaire.   *uhn deek-syawn-NEHR*

1228. Guide book.   Un guide.   *uhn gheed*

1229. Newspaper.   Un journal.   *uhn zhoor-NAHL*

1230. Magazine.   Un magazine.   *uhn mah-gah-ZEEN*

1231. Postcards.   Des cartes postales.
day kahrt paws-TAHL

1232. Greeting cards.   Des cartes de vœux.
day kahrt duh VUH

1233. Envelopes.   Des enveloppes.   *day zahn-vuh-LAWP*

1234. Pencil.   Un crayon.   *uhn kreh-YAWN*

1235. Pen.   Un stylo.   *uhn stee-LOH*

1236. Eraser.   Une gomme. / Un efface (Quebec).
ewn gawm / uhn eh-FAHS

1237. Scissors.   Des ciseaux.   *day SEE-soh*

1238. Notepad.   Un bloc-notes.   *uhn blawk-NAWT*

1239. Stapler.   Une agrafeuse.   *ew nah-grah-FUHZ*

1240. Staple.   Une agrafe.   *ew nah-GRAHF*

1241. Paper clip.   Un trombone.   *uhn trawn-BAWNN*

1242. Rubber band.   Une élastique.   *uh NAY-lahs-TEEK*

1243. Highlighter. Un surligneur. *uhn SEWR-leen-YUHR*

1244. Correction fluid. Un correcteur liquide.
uhn kaw-rehk-TUHR lee-KEED

1245. Ruler. Une règle. / Une latte (Belgium).
ewn REH-gluh / ewn laht

1246. Tissue paper. Le papier de soie.
luh pah-PYAY duh swah

1247. Wrapping paper. Le papier d'emballage.
luh pah-PYAY dahn-bah-LAHZH

At the Tobacconist's / *Au Tabac*

1248. Where is the nearest tobacconist's?
Où est le bureau de tabac le prus proche?
oo eh luh BEW-roh duh ta-BAH luh plew prawsh

1249. I want some cigarettes / cigars.
Je veux des cigarettes / des cigares.
zhuh vuh day see-gah-REHT / day see-GAHR

1250. I need a lighter / some matches.
Il me faut un briquet / des allumettes.
eel muh foh uh BREE-keh / day zah-lew-MEHT

1251. A pack of cigarettes. Un paquet de cigarettes.
uh pah-KEH duh see-gah-REHT

1252. Stamps. Les timbres. *lay TEHN-bruh*

1253. Lottery tickets. Les tickets de loto.
lay TEE-keh duh loh-TOH

At the Hair Salon / *Chez le Coiffeur*

1254. Where is there a good hair salon?
Où se trouve un bon coiffeur?
oo suh troov uhn bawn kwah-FUHR

1255. I need to get my hair cut (dyed).
J'ai besoin de me faire couper (faire teindre) les cheveux.
zhay buh-zwehn duh muh fehr KOO-pay (fehr TEHN-druh) lay shuh-VUH

1256. Not too short. Pas trop court. *pah troh koor*

1257. Do not cut any off the top.
N'en coupez pas sur le dessus.
nahn KOO-pay pah sewr luh duh-SEW

1258. I part my hair on the side / on the other side.
Je fais ma raie sur le côté / sur l'autre côté.
zhuh feh mah ray sewr luh koh-TAY / sewr LOH-truh koh-TAY

1259. In the middle. Au milieu. *oh mee-LYUH*

1260. The water is too hot / cold.
L'eau est trop chaude / froide.
loh eh troh shohd / frwahd

1261. I want a shampoo. Je veux un shampooing.
zhuh vuh zuhn shahn-PWEHN

1262. A haircut. Une coupe. *ewn koop*

1263. A hair dye. Une couleur. *ewn koo-LUHR*

117

1264. A blow dry.   Un brushing.   *uhn BRUHSH-eeng*

1265. Finger wave.   Une mise en pli.   *ewn mee zahn PLEE*

1266. Perm.   Une permanente.   *ewn pehr-ma-NAHNT*

1267. Layered.   Dégradé.   *day-grah-DAY*

1268. Streaks/Lowlights.   Des mèches.   *day mesh*

1269. Highlights.   Des balayages.   *day bah-lay-AHZH*

1270. Manicure.   Une manucure.   *ewn mah-new-KEWR*

1271. Pedicure.   Une pédicurie.   *ewn pay-dee-kew-ree*

Laundry and Dry Cleaning / La Blanchisserie et le Pressing

1272. Laundromat.
   Une laverie. / Une launderette (Quebec).
   ewn lah-VREE. / ewn lohn-DREHT

1273. Dry cleaner's.   Un pressing. / Un nettoyeur (Quebec).
   uhn PREH-seeng. / uhn neh-twah-YUHR

1274. Laundry service.   Une blanchisserie.
   ewn blahn-shees-REE

1275. Laundry room (in a home).   Une buanderie.
   ewn bew-ahn-DREE

1276. To be washed / cleaned / mended / pressed.
   À faire laver / nettoyer / repriser / repasser.
   ah fehr lah-VAY / neh-twah-YAY / ruh-pree-ZAY / ruh-pah-SAY

1277. Do I need coins or tokens for these machines?
Il faut des pièces ou des jetons pour ces machines?
eel foh day pee-EHS oo day zhuh-TAWN poor say mah-SHEEN

1278. Where can I buy some detergent?
Où peut-on acheter de la lessive?
oo puh-taw nahsh-tay duh lah leh-SEEV

1279. When will my things be ready?
Quand est-ce que mes affaires seront prêtes?
kahn tehs-kuh may-zah-FEHR suh-RAWN preht

1280. Can you iron these shirts?
Pouvez-vous faire repasser ces chemises?
poo-vay-voo fehr ruh-pah-SAY say shuh-MEEZ

1281. Can you hem these pants?
Pouvez-vous raccourcir ce pantalon?
poo-vay-voo rah-koor-SEER suh pahn-tah-LAWN

HEALTH

Accidents / Les Accidents

1282. There has been an accident.   Il y a eu un accident.
eel-ya ew uh nak-see-DAHN

1283. Get a doctor.   Chercher un médecin.
shehr-SHAY uhn mayd-SEHN

1284. Call an ambulance.   Appeler une ambulance.
ah-PLAY ew nahn-bew-LAHNS

1285. Please take him to the hospital/the emergency room.
Veuillez l'emmener à l'hôpital / la salle d'urgences.
*vuh-yay lahm-NAY ah loh-pee-TAHL / lah sahl
dewr-ZHAHNS*

1286. Help!   Au secours! À l'aide!   *ohs-KOOR! ah LEHD!*

1287. We need a stretcher.
Il nous faut une civière / un brancard.
eel noo foh ewn see-VYEHR / uhn brahn-KAHR

1288. Give him/her some water.   Donnez-lui de l'eau.
DAW-nay-LWEE duh loh

1289. He is (seriously) injured.   Il est (gravement) blessé.
eel eh (GRAHV-mahn) bleh-SAY

1290. Help me carry her.   Aidez-moi à la porter.
EH-day-mwah ah lah pawr-TAY

1291. He was knocked down.   On l'a renversé.
awn lah RAHN-vehr-SAY

1292. She has fallen/fainted.
Elle est tombée / s'est évanouie.
ehl eh tawn-BAY / seh-TAY-vah-nooh-EE

1293. He has a fracture/bruise/cut.
Il a une fracture / un bleu / une coupure.
eel ah ewn frahk-TEWR / uhn bluh / ewn koo-PEWR

1294. She has burned/cut her hand.
Elle s'est brûlé / s'est coupé la main.
ehl seh brew-LAY / seh koo-PAY lah mehn

1295. It is just a scratch.   C'est seulement une égratignure.
seh SUHL-mahn ewn EY-grah-teen-YEWR

Quick & to the Point

Accidents / Les Accidents

Are you all right?
Ça va?   *sah vah*

It hurts here.
Ça me fait mal ici.
sah muh feh mahl ee-SEE

I feel weak.
Je me sens faible.
zhuh muh sahn FEH-bluh

I feel nauseated.
J'ai mal au coeur.
zhay mahl oh kuhr

I feel like throwing up.
J'ai envie de vomir.
zhay ahn-vee duh voh-meer

I cannot move my hand.
Je ne peux pas bouger la main.
zhuh nuh puh pah boo-zhay lah MEHN.

I have hurt my leg.
Je me suis fait mal à la jambe.
zhuh muh swee feh mahl ah lah ZHANB

It is bleeding.
Ça saigne.
sah SEHNN-yuh

121

1296. It is swollen / infected.   C'est enflé / infecté.
seh tahn-FLAY / tehn-fehk-TAY

1297. Do you have any bandages?
Avez-vous des pansements?
ah-vay-voo day pahns-MAHN

1298. Can you bandage this wound?
Pouvez-vous panser cette blessure?
poo-vay-voo pahn-SAY seht blehs-SEWR

1299. I need something for a tourniquet.
Il me faut quelque chose pour un tourniquet.
eel muh foh kehl-kuh-SHOHZ poor uhn toor-nee-KEH

1300. I want to sit down a moment.
Je veux m'asseoir un moment.
zhuh vuh mah-swahr uhn maw-mahn

1301. I have a headache.   J'ai mal à la tête.
zhay mah lah lah teht

1302. I have a stomachache.   J'ai mal au ventre.
zhay mah loh vahn-truh

1303. I have an earache.   J'ai mal à l'oreille.
zhay mah lah law-ray

Illness / La Maladie

1304. I want to see a doctor / specialist.
Je veux voir un médecin / un spécialiste.
zhuh vuh vwahr uhn mayd-SEHN / uhn
spay-see-ah-LEEST

1305. An English-speaking doctor.
Un médecin qui parle anglais.
uhn mayd-SEHN kee pahrl ahn-GLEH

1306. I am very sick. Je suis très malade.
zhuh swee treh mah-LAHD

1307. I do not sleep well. Je ne dors pas bien.
zhuh nuh dawr pah byehn

1308. I'm having intestinal problems.
J'ai des problèmes intestinaux.
zhay day praw-BLEHM ehn-tehs-tee-NOH

1309. I'm allergic to penicillin.
Je suis allergique à la pénicilline.
zhuh swee zah-lehr-ZHEEK ah lah pay-nee-see-LEEN

1310. I am diabetic. Je suis diabétique.
zhuh swee dee-ah-bay-TEEK

1311. I'm pregnant. Je suis enceinte.
zhuh swee zahn-SEHNT

1312. I'm on the pill. Je prends la pilule.
zhuh prahn lah pee-LEWL

1313. I have high blood pressure.
J'ai une hypertension artérielle.
zhay ewn ee-pehr-tahn-syawn ahr-tay-ree-ELL

1314. Appendicitis. L'appendicite. *lah-pahn-dee-SEET*

1315. An animal bite. Une morsure. *ewn mawr-SEWR*

1316. An insect bite. Une piqûre. *ewn pee-KEWR*

1317. A blister. Une ampoule. *ewn ahn-POOL*

1318. A boil. Un furoncle. *uhn few-RAWN-kluh*

1319. A burn. Une brûlure. *ewn brew-LEWR*

1320. Chills. Un coup de froid. *uhn koo duh frwah*

1321. A cold. Un rhume. *uhn rewm*

1322. Constipation. La constipation.
lah kawn-stee-pah-SYAWN

1323. A cough. Une toux. *ewn tooh*

1324. A cramp. Une crampe. *ewn krahmp*

1325. Diarrhea. La diarrhée. *lah dee-ah-RAY*

1326. Dysentery. La dysenterie. *la dee-sahn-TREE*

1327. An earache. Une otite. *ew naw-TEET*

1328. A fever. Une fièvre. *ewn fee-EHV-ruh*

1329. The flu. La grippe. *la greep*

1330. Food poisoning. Une intoxication alimentaire.
ew nehn-tawk-see-kah-SYAWN ah-lee-mahn-TEHR

1331. Hives. L'urticaire. *lewr-tee-KEHR*

1332. Hypothermia. L'hypothermie. *lee-paw-tehr-MEE*

1333. Indigestion. L'indigestion. *lehn-dee-zhehs-TYAWN*

1334. Menstrual cramps. Les règles douleureuses.
lay REHG-luh doo-luh-RUHZ

1335. A migraine. Une migraine. *ewn mee-GREHNN*

1336. Nausea. La nausée. *lah noh-ZAY*

1337. Pneumonia. La pneumonie. *lah pnuh-maw-NEE*

1338. A rash.   Une éruption cutanée.
ewn ay-rewp-SYAWN kew-tah-NAY

1339. A runny nose.   Le nez qui coule.   *luh nay kee kool*

1340. A sore throat.   Un mal de gorge.
uhn mal duh gawrzh

1341. A sprain.   Une entorse.   *ew nahn-TAWRS*

1342. A sunburn.   Un coup de soleil.
uhn koo duh soh-LAY

1343. Sunstroke.   L'insolation.   *lehn-saw-lah-SYAWN*

1344. Stomach flu (gastroenteritis).   La gastro.
lah GAH-stroh

1345. A stuffy nose.   Le nez bouché.   *luh nay boo-SHAY*

1346. Tonsilitis.   Une angine. / Une amygdalite (Quebec).
ew nahn-ZHEEN / ew nah-mee-dah-LEET

1347. What should I do?   Que dois-je faire?
kuh dwah-zhuh fehr

1348. Must I stay in bed?   Dois-je rester au lit?
dwah-zhuh reh-STAY oh lee

1349. Do I need antibiotics?
Dois-je prendre des antibiotiques?
dwah-zhuh PRAHN-druh day zahn-tee-bee-aw-TEEK

1350. I feel better.   Je me sens mieux.
zhuh muh sahn myuh

1351. I need a receipt for my health insurance.
Il me faut un reçu pour l'assurance.
eel muh foh uhn ruh-SEW poor lah-sew-RAHNS

1352. Medicine.   Des médicaments.
day may-deek-ah-MAHN

1353. A pill / a tablet.   Un comprimé / un cachet.
uhn kawn-pree-MAY / uhn KAH-shay

1354. A prescription.   Une ordonnance.
ew nawr-daw-nahns

1355. Suppository.   Un suppositoire.
uhn sew-paw-zee-TWAHR

1356. Ointment.   Une pommade.   *ewn paw-MAHD*

1357. Side effects.   Les effets secondaires.
lay zay-FAY suh-kawn-DEHR

1358. A drop.   Une goutte.   *ewn goot*

1359. A teaspoonful.   Une cuillerée.
ewn KWEE-yehr-AY

1360. Hot water.   De l'eau chaude.   *duh loh showhd*

1361. Ice.   De la glace.   *duh lah glahs*

1362. Every hour.   Toutes les heures.   *toot lay zuhr*

1363. Before (after) meals.   Avant (après) les repas.
ah-VAHN (ah-PREH) lay ruh-PAH

1364. Twice a day.   Deux fois par jour.
duh fwah pahr zhoor

1365. On going to bed.   En se couchant.
ahn suh koo-SHAHN

1366. On getting up.   En se levant.   *ahn suh luh-VAHN*

1367. X-rays.   Les radios.   *lay rah-DYOH*

1368. Blood test.   Une prise de sang.   *ewn preez duh sahn*

1369. Screening.   Le dépistage.   *luh DAY-pees-TAHZH*

Pharmacy / *La Pharmacie*

1370. Is there an English-speaking pharmacy near here?
Y a-t-il une pharmacie où l'on comprend l'anglais près d'ici?
yah-tee lewn far-ma-SEE oo lawn kawn-PRAHN lahn-GLEH preh dee-SEE

1371. Where is there a 24-hour pharmacy?
Où y a-t-il une pharmacie qui soit ouverte 24 heures?
oo ee-yah-TEE lewn far-ma-SEE kee swah too-VEHRT vehn-kah-TRUHR

1372. Can you fill this prescription?
Pouvez-vous remplir cette ordonnance?
poo-vay-voo rahn-PLEER seht awr-daw-NAHNS

1373. How long will it take?
Combien de temps vous faudra-t-il?
kawn-BYEHN duh tahn voo foh-drah-TEEL

1374. I need some adhesive tape.
J'ai besoin du sparadrap.
zhay buh-ZWEHN dew spah-rah-DRAH

1375. Antiseptic.   L'antiseptique.   *lahn-tee-sehp-TEEK*

1376. Aspirin.   L'aspirine.   *las-pee-REEN*

1377. Bandages.   Des bandages.   *day bahn-DAHZH*

1378. Band-Aids™.   Des pansements.   *day pahns-MAHN*

1379. A cleanser. Un nettoyant. *uhn neh-twah-YAHN*

1380. A comb. Un peigne. *uhn PEHNN-yuh*

1381. Condoms. Des préservatifs.
day pray-zehr-vah-TEEF

1382. Contact lens solution.
La solution d'entretien pour lentilles.
*lah saw-loo-SYAWN dahn-truh-TYEHN poor
lahn-TEE-yuh*

1383. Cotton. Le coton. *luh koh-TAWN*

1384. Dental floss. Le fil dentaire. *luh feel dahn-TEHR*

1385. Deodorant. Le déodorant. *luh day-oh-doh-RAHN*

1386. Diapers. Des couches. *day koosh*

1387. Earplugs. Des bouchons d'oreille.
day boo-SHAWN doh-RAY

1388. Gauze. De la gaze. *duh lah gahz*

1389. A hair brush. Une brosse à cheveux.
ewn braws ah shuh-VUH

1390. A hearing aid. Un appareil acoustique.
uhn ah-pah-RAY ah-koos-TEEK

1391. A hot water bottle. Une bouillote. *ewn
boo-ee-YAWT*

1392. An ice bag. Un sac à glace. *uhn sahk ah GLAHSS*

1393. Insect bite lotion.
La lotion contre les piqûres d'insecte.
law-SYAWN KAWN-truh day pee-KEWR dehn-SEHKT

1394. Insect repellent. Un produit anti-insecte.
uhn praw-DWEE AHN-tee-ehn-SEHKT

1395. Iodine. De l'iode. *duh lee-OHD*

1396. A laxative. Un laxatif. *uhn lak-sah-TEEF*

1397. Lipstick. Le rouge à lèvres. *luh roozh ah LEHV-ruh*

1398. Makeup. Le maquillage. *luh mah-kee-AHZH*

1399. A medicine dropper. Un compte-gouttes.
uhn kawnt-GOOT

1400. Mouthwash. Le bain de bouche. *luh behn duh boosh*

1401. A nail file. Une lime à ongles.
ewn leem ah AWN-gluh

1402. Nail clippers. Des coupe-ongles.
day koop-AWN-gluh

1403. Nail-polish remover. Le dissolvant.
luh dee-sawl-VAHN

1404. Perfume. Le parfum. *luh pahr-FEHN*

1405. A razor. Un rasoir. *uhn rah-ZWAHR*

1406. Razor blades. Des lames de rasoir.
day lahm duh rah-ZWAHR

1407. Rubbing alcohol. De l'alcool dénaturé.
duh lahl-KOHL DAY-nah-tew-RAY

1408. Sanitary napkins. Des serviettes hygiéniques.
day sehr-VYEHT ee-zhee-ay-NEEK

1409. Shampoo. Le shampooing. *luh shahn-PWEHN*

1410. Shaving cream (mousse).
La crème (mousse) à raser.
lah krehm (moos) ah rah-ZAY

1411. Sleeping pills.   Des somnifères.   *day sawm-nee-FEHR*

1412. Sunblock.   L'écran solaire.   *lay-KRAH<u>N</u> saw-LEHR*

1413. Sunburn ointment.   La lotion après-soleil.
lah law-SYAW<u>N</u> ah-preh-saw-LAY

1414. Tampons.   Des tampons.   *day tah<u>n</u>-PAW<u>N</u>*

1415. A thermometer.   Un thermomètre.
uh<u>n</u> tehr-maw-MEH-truh

1416. Tissues.   Des mouchoirs.   *day moo-SHWAHR*

Pharmacies / Les pharmacies

It is not possible to browse the aisles for over-the-counter medication in European pharmacies because all of the medication is actually stored behind the counter. You must ask the pharmacist for a specific type of medicine or explain your symptoms. Pharmacies are marked by a green cross above the door, and at least one pharmacy in each city is open 24 hours for emergencies. Often there is a list available of which pharmacy is open as the *pharmacie de garde* for a certain night, or you can consult the yellow pages.

1417. Toothbrush.   Une brosse à dents.
   ewn braws ah dahn

1418. Toothpaste.   Le dentifrice.   *luh dahn-tee-FREESS*

1419. Vitamins.   Des vitamines.   *day vee-tah-MEEN*

1420. Wipes.   Des lingettes.   *day lehn-ZHEHT*

Dentist / *Le Dentiste*

1421. Do you know a good dentist?
   Connaissez-vous un bon dentiste?
   kaw-neh-say-voo uhn bawn dahn-TEEST

1422. I have a toothache.   J'ai mal aux dents.
   zhay mahl oh dahn

1423. I think I have a cavity.   Je pense que j'ai une carie.
   zhuh pahns kuh zhay ewn KAH-ree

1424. Can you fix it (temporarily)?
   Pouvez-vous l'arranger (temporairement)?
   poo-vay-voo lah-rahn-ZHAY (tahn-poh-rehr-MAHN)

1425. I have lost a filling.   J'ai perdu un plombage.
   zhay pehr-DEW uhn plawn-BAHZH

1426. I have a broken tooth.   Je me suis cassé une dent.
   zhuh muh swee kah-SAY ewn dahn

1427. I do not want it extracted.
   Je ne veux pas la faire arracher.
   zhuh nuh vuh pah lah fehr ah-rah-SHAY

1428. You are hurting me.   Vous me faites mal.
   voo muh feht mahl

1429. Cleaning.   Le détartrage.   *luh DAY-tahr-TRAHZH*

1430. Local anesthesia.   Une anesthésie locale.
ew nah-neh-stay-ZEE law-KAHL

1431. Gums.   Les gencives.   *lay zhah<u>n</u>-SEEV*

1432. Nerve.   Le nerf.   *luh nehr*

1433. Jaw.   La mâchoire.   *lah mah-SHWAHR*

1434. Cavity.   Une carie.   *ewn KAH-ree*

1435. Crown.   Une couronne.   *ewn koo-RAWNN*

1436. Root canal.   Un canal dentaire.
uh<u>n</u> kah-NAHL dah<u>n</u>-TEHR

1437. Dentures.   Le dentier.   *luh dah<u>n</u>-TYAY*

1438. Braces.   L'appareil dentaire.
lah-pah-RAY dah<u>n</u>-TEHR

1439. Baby teeth.   Les dents de lait.   *lay dah<u>n</u> duh leh*

1440. Wisdom teeth.   Les dents de sagesse.
lay dah<u>n</u> duh sah-ZHEHS

Optician / *L'Opticien*

1441. Where can I get my glasses fixed?
Où est-ce je peux faire réparer mes lunettes?
oo ehs-kuh zhuh puh fehr ray-pah-RAY may lew-NEHT

1442. The frames are broken.   La monture est cassée.
lah maw<u>n</u>-TEWR eh kah-SAY

1443. I need some contact-lens solution.
J'ai besoin de la solution pour lentilles.
zhay buh-zwehn duh lah saw-lew-SYAW<u>N</u> poor
lah<u>n</u>-TEE-yuh

1444. Soft (hard) contact lens.   Les lentilles souples (dures).
lay lah<u>n</u>-TEE-yuh SOO-pluh (dewr)

1445. Disposable contacts.   Les lentilles jetables.
lay lah<u>n</u>-TEE-yuh zhuh-TAH-bluh

1446. I've lost my glasses case (contacts case).
J'ai perdu mon étui de lunettes (de lentilles).
zhay pehr-DEW maw<u>n</u> ay-TWEE duh lew-NEHT (duh
lah<u>n</u>-TEE-yuh)

1447. I would like some eye drops.
Je voudrais des gouttes pour les yeux.
zhuh voo-DREH day goot poor lay zyuh

1448. Near-sighted.   Myope.   mee-YAWP

1449. Far-sighted.   Hypermétrope.   ee-pehr-may-TRAWP

1450. Clear.   Net.   neht

1451. Blurry.   Flou.   floo

Parts of the Body / Les Parties du Corps

1452. Ankle.   La cheville.   lah shuh-VEE-yuh

1453. Appendix.   L'appendice.   lah-pah<u>n</u>-DEES

1454. Arm.   Le bras.   luh brah

1455. Back.   Le dos.   luh doh

1456. Belly.   Le ventre.   *luh VAHN-truh*

1457. Blood.   Le sang.   *luh sahn*

1458. Bone.   L'os.   *lawss*

1459. Bones.   Les os.   *lay zoh*

1460. Cheek.   La joue.   *lah zhoo*

1461. Chest.   La poitrine.   *lah pwa-TREEN*

1462. Chin.   Le menton.   *luh mahn-TAWN*

1463. Collar bone.   La clavicule.   *lah klah-vee-KEWL*

1464. Ear.   L'oreille.   *law-RAY*

1465. Elbow.   Le coude.   *luh kood*

1466. Eye.   L'œil.   *LUH-yee*

1467. Eyes.   Les yeux.   *lay zyuh*

1468. Eyebrows.   Les sourcils.   *lay soor-SEE*

1469. Eyelashes.   Les cils.   *lay seel*

1470. Eyelid.   La paupière.   *lah poh-PYEHR*

1471. Face.   Le visage.   *luh vee-ZAHZH*

1472. Finger.   Le doigt.   *luh dwah*

1473. Fist.   Le poing.   *luh pwahn*

1474. Foot.   Le pied.   *luh pyay*

1475. Forehead.   Le front.   *luh frawn*

1476. Hair.   Les cheveux.   *lay shuh-VUH*

1477. Hand.   La main.   *lah mehn*

1478. Head.   La tête.   *lah teht*

1479. Heart.   Le cœur.   *luh kuhr*

1480. Heel.   Le talon.   *luh tah-LAWN*

1481. Hip.   La hanche.   *lah ahnsh*

1482. Intestines.   Les intestins.   *lay zehn-teh-STEHN*

1483. Jaw.   La mâchoire.   *lah mah-SHWAHR*

1484. Joint.   L'articulation.   *lahr-tee-kew-lah-SYAWN*

1485. Kidney.   Le rein.   *luh rehn*

1486. Knee.   Le genou.   *luh zhuh-NOO*

1487. Knuckle.   L'articulation du doigt.
   lahr-tee-kew-lah-SYAWN dew dwah

1488. Leg.   La jambe.   *lah zhahmb*

1489. Lip.   La lèvre.   *lah LEHV-ruh*

1490. Liver.   Le foie.   *luh fwah*

1491. Lung.   Le poumon.   *luh poo-mawn*

1492. Mouth.   La bouche.   *lah boosh*

1493. Muscle.   Le muscle.   *luh MEWS-kluh*

1494. Nail.   L'ongle.   *LAWN-gluh*

1495. Neck.   Le cou.   *luh koo*

1496. Nerve.   Le nerf.   *luh nehr*

1497. Nose.   Le nez.   *luh nay*

1498. Rib.   La côte.   *lah koht*

1499. Shoulder.   L'épaule.   *lay-POHL*

1500. Side (left, right).   Le côté (droit, gauche).
   luh koh-TAY (drwah, gohsh)

1501. Skin. La peau. *lah poh*

1502. Skull. Le crâne. *luh krahnn*

1503. Spine. La colonne vertébrale.
lah kaw-LAWNN vehr-tay-BRAHL

1504. Stomach. L'estomac. *lehs-taw-MAH*

1505. Tooth. La dent. *lah dahn*

1506. Thigh. La cuisse. *lah kweess*

1507. Throat. La gorge. *lah gawrzh*

1508. Thumb. Le pouce. *luh pooss*

1509. Toe. L'orteil. *lawr-TAY*

1510. Tongue. La langue. *lah lahng*

1511. Tonsils. Les amygdales. *lay zah-mee-dahl*

1512. Waist. La taille. *lah TY-uh*

1513. Wrist. Le poignet. *luh pwahn-YAY*

COMMUNICATION

Bank / *La Banque*

1514. Where is the nearest bank?
Où est la banque le plus proche d'ici?
oo eh lah bahnk luh plew prawsh dee-SEE

1515. Is there a currency exchange office?
Est-ce qu'il y a un bureau de change?
ess-keel-YA uhn bew-roh duh shahnzh

1516. I'm looking for an ATM.

Je cherche un distributeur automatique.

zhuh shehrsh uhn dee-stree-bew-TUHR oh-taw-mah-TEEK

1517. I need to withdraw some cash.

J'ai besoin de retirer de l'argent.

zhay buh-zwehn duh ruh-tee-RAY duh lahr-ZHAHN

1518. I would like to exchange some traveler's checks.

Je voudrais échanger des chèques de voyage.

zhuh voo-DREH ay-shahn-ZHAY day shehk duh vwah-YAHZH

1519. What is the exchange rate from U.S. dollars to Euros?

Quel est le taux d'échange entre le dollar américain et l'euro?

kehl eh luh toh day-SHAHNZH AHN-truh luh daw-LAHR ah-may-ree-KEHN ay luh-ROH

1520. Swiss francs.   Les francs suisses.   *les frahn sweess*

1521. Canadian dollars.   Les dollars canadiens.

lay daw-LAHR kah-nah-DYEHN

1522. May I have small bills?

Puis-je avoir des petits billets?

PWEE-zhuh ah-vwahr day puh-TEE bee-YAY

1523. May I have some change?

Puis-je avoir de la monnaie?

PWEE-zhuh ah-vwahr duh lah maw-NAY

Post Office / *La Poste*

1524. Where is the post office?   Où est la poste?
oo eh la pawst

1525. What is the price of stamps?
Quel est le tarif des timbres?
kehl eh luh tah-REEF day TEHN-bruh

1526. For postcards.   Pour les cartes postales.
poor lay kahrt paw-STAHL

1527. For letters.   Pour les lettres.   *poor lay LEH-truh*

1528. I would like five stamps for the United States.
Je voudrais cinq timbres pour les États-Unis.
zhuh voo-DREH sehnk TEHN-bruh poor lay zay-TAH-zew-NEE

1529. By airmail.   Par avion.   *pahr ah-VYAWN*

1530. Registered.   Recommandé.   *ruh-kaw-mahn-DAY*

1531. Insured.   Valeur déclarée.   *vah-LUHR day-klah-RAY*

1532. Mailbox.   Une boîte à lettres.   *ewn bwaht ah LEH-truh*

1533. Post-office box.
Une boîte postale. / Une case postale (Switzerland).
ewn bwaht paw-STAHL / ewn kahz paw-STAHL

1534. Is it possible to send money to the United States?
Est-ce possible d'envoyer de l'argent aux États-Unis?
ehs paw-SEE-bluh dahn-vwah-YAY duh lahr-ZHAHN oh zay-TAH-zew-NEE

1535. I want to send a money order/a package.

Je veux envoyer un mandat / un colis.

zhuh vuh ahn-vwah-YAY uhn mahn-DAH / uhn kaw-LEE

1536. May I have a receipt, please?

Puis-je avoir un ticket de caisse, s'il vous plaît?

PWEE-zhuh ah-vwahr uhn TEE-keh duh kehss, seel voo pleh

1537. When will it arrive? Quand va-t-il arriver?

kahn vah-TEEL ah-ree-VAY

Telephone / Le Téléphone

1538. I'd like to buy a cell phone.

J'aimerais acheter un téléphone portable / un cellulaire (Quebec) / un natel (Switzerland).

*zhehm-reh ahsh-tay uhn tay-lay-FAWNN pawr-
TAH-bluh / uhn seh-lew-LEHR / uhn nah-TEHL*

1539. Is there a contract or fixed rate plan?

Y a-t-il un contrat ou forfait?

ee-yah-TEEL uhn kawn-TRAH oo fawr-FEH

1540. I prefer a prepaid plan with no subscription.

Je préfère les cartes prépayés sans engagement.

*zhuh pray-FEHR lay kahrt pray-pay-YAY sahn
zahn-gazh-MAHN*

1541. I have to buy more credit for my cell phone.

Je dois recharger le crédit pour mon téléphone
portable.

*zhuh dwah ruh-shahr-zhay luh kray-DEE poor mawn
tay-lay-FAWNN pawr-TAH-bluh*

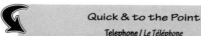

Quick & to the Point

Telephone / Le Téléphone

fixed rate	le forfait	luh fawr-FEH
prepaid	prépayé(e)	pray-pay-yay
unlimited	illimité(e)	ee-lee-mee-TAY
text message	le SMS / le texto	luh ehs-ehm-ehs / luh tehks-toh
voicemail	la messagerie vocale	lah meh-sahzh-ree vaw-KAHL
call waiting	le double appel	luh doo blah-PEHL
caller ID	la présentation du numéro	lah pray-zahn-tah-SYAWN dew new-may-ROH
SIM card	la carte SIM	lah kahrt SEEM
PIN code	le code secret	luh kohd suh-kreh
locked	bloqué(e)	blaw-kay
unlocked	débloqué(e)	day-blaw-kay
ringtone	la sonnerie	lah sawn-ree

1542. My cell phone does not work here.

Mon portable ne fonctionne pas ici.

mawn pawr-TAH-bluh nuh fawnk-syawnn pah zee-SEE

1543. I don't have a SIM card.   Je n'ai pas de carte SIM.

zhuh nay pah duh kahrt SEEM

1544. I need to recharge the battery.

J'ai besoin de recharger la batterie.

zhay buh-zwehn duh ruh-shahr-ZHAY la bah-TREE

1545. I'd like to buy a phone card, please.
Une télécarte, s'il vous plaît.
ewn tay-lay-KAHRT seel voo pleh

1546. Do you have a phone book? Avez-vous un annuaire?
ah-vay-voo uh NAH-new-EHR

1547. Where can I make a telephone call?
Où est-ce que je peux téléphoner?
OO ehs-kuh zhuh puh tay-lay-faw-NAY

1548. I want to make a local / international / collect call.
Je veux faire un appel local / international / en PCV.
zhuh vuh fehr uh nah-PEHL law-KAHL / ehn-tehr-nah-syaw-NAHL / ahn pay-say-vay

1549. How much does it cost to call the United States?
C'est combien pour appeler les États-Unis?
seh kawn-byehn poor ah-PLAY lay zay-TAH-zew-NEE

1550. What is the number here?
Quel est le numéro de téléphone ici?
kehl eh luh new-may-roh duh tay-lay-FAWNN ee-SEE

1551. Do you have the number for the American consulate?
Avez-vous le numéro de téléphone pour le consulat américain?
ah-vay-voo luh new-may-roh duh tay-lay-FAWNN poor luh kawn-sew-LAH ah-may-ree-KEHN

1552. There is a telephone call for you.
Il y a un appel pour vous.
eel-yah uh nah-PEHL poor VOO

1553. Hello. Allô. *ah-LOH*

1554. There is no answer. Personne ne répond.
pehr-SAWNN nuh ray-PAWN

1555. It's busy. C'est occupé. *seh taw-kew-PAY*

1556. Please hold. Ne quittez pas. *nuh KEE-tay PAH*

1557. May I speak to ___? Puis-je parler à ___?
PWEE-zhuh pahr-LAY ah

1558. He is not here. Il n'est pas ici. *eel neh pah zee-SEE*

1559. Would you like to leave a message?
Voulez-vous laisser un message?
voo-lay-voo lehs-say uhn meh-SAHZH

1560. Can I leave a message for ___?
Je peux laisser un message pour ___?
zhuh puh leh-say uhn meh-ZAHZH poor

1561. My number is ___. Mon numéro est ___.
maw new-may-ROH eh

1562. Who is calling? C'est de la part de qui?
seh duh lah pahr duh KEE

1563. This is ___ speaking. C'est ___ à l'appareil.
seh ___ ah lah-pah-RAY

1564. I'll put you through to him/her.
Je vous le/la passe. *zhuh voo luh/lah pahss*

1565. One moment, please. Un instant, s'il vous plaît.
uhn ehn-STAHN seel voo pleh

1566. Please hold on. Patientez, s'il vous plaît.
pah-syahn-TAY seel voo pleh

1567. Can you call back?   Pouvez-vous rappeler?
poo-vay-voo rah-PLAY

1568. I'll call back later.   Je vais rappeler plus tard.
zhuh veh rah-play plew tahr

1569. We were cut off.   Nous avons été coupés.
noo-zah-vaw<u>n</u> ay-TAY koo-PAY

Telephone numbers / Les numéros de téléphone

In order to call a European country from the U.S. or Canada, you must first dial the exit code 011 and then the country code before the telephone number: 33 for France, 32 for Belgium and 41 for Switzerland. The plus sign (+) can replace the exit code when calling from a cell phone.

French telephone numbers begin with 0; however, this 0 is only used when calling within France. When dialing internationally, you must drop the 0 between the country code and telephone number. Therefore the telephone number for the American Embassy in Paris must be dialed 01 43 12 22 22 when calling from France, but +33 1 43 12 22 22 when calling from outside of France.

Computers and Internet / *Les Ordinateurs et Internet*

1570. Is there a computer here that I may use?
Est-ce qu'il y a un ordinateur ici que je peux utiliser?
ess-kee-Iyah uh nawr-dee-nah-TUHR ee-SEE kuh zhuh puh ew-tee-lee-ZAY

1571. Do you have free wireless Internet?
Avez-vous le Wi-Fi gratuit?
ah-vay-voo luh wee-fee grah-TWEE

1572. Do I need a password?
Est-ce qu'il faut un mot de passe?
ehs-keel foh uhn moh duh pahss

1573. Where is the nearest Internet café?
Où est le cybercafé le plus proche?
oo eh luh SEE-behr-kah-FEH luh plew prawsh

1574. I want to check my e-mail.
Je veux regarder mon courriel / mes mails.
zhuh vuh ruh-gahr-DAY mawn koo-RYEHL / may mehl

1575. I'd like to update my blog.
Je voudrais mettre à jour mon blog.
zhuh voo-dreh MEH-truh ah zhoor mawn BLAWG

1576. Can I access Facebook / Twitter / Myspace?
Puis-je acceder à mon compte
Facebook / Twitter / Myspace?
PWEE-zhuh ahk-say-day ah mawn kawnt fays-boohk / TWEE-tuhr / MY-spehs

1577. Do you have a QWERTY keyboard?
Avez-vous un clavier QWERTY?
ah-vay-voo uhn klah-VYAY kwehr-TEE

1578. Can I plug in my flash drive?
Puis-je brancher ma clé USB?
PWEE-zhuh brahn-shay mah klay ew-ehs-BAY

1579. Where is the @ sign?   Où se trouve l'arobase?
oo suh troov lah-roh-BAHZ

1580. I forgot my password.   J'ai oublié mon mot de passe.
zhay oo-blee-ay mawn moh duh PAHSS

1581. The screen is frozen.   L'écran est bloqué.
lay-KRAHN eh blaw-KAY

1582. How much does it cost to print one page?
Il coûte combien pour imprimer une page?
eel koot kawn-BYEHN poor ehn-pree-MAY ewn PAHZH

1583. I need to download / print a document.
J'ai besoin de télécharger / d'imprimer un document.
zhay buh-zwehn duh tay-lay-shahr-ZHAY / dehn-pree-MAY uhn daw-kew-MAHN

1584. May I send a fax / make some photocopies?
Puis-je envoyer un fax / faire des photocopies?
PWEE-zhuh ahn-vwah-yay uhn FAHKS / fehr day foh-toh-kaw-PEE

1585. Desktop computer.   Un ordinateur de bureau.
uhn awr-dee-nah-TUHR duh bew-ROH

1586. Laptop computer.   Un ordinateur portable.
uhn awr-dee-nah-TUHR pawr-TAH-bluh

145

1587. Printer.   Une imprimante.   *ew nehn-pree-MAHNT*

1588. Ink cartridge.   Une cartouche d'encre.
ewn kahr-TOOSH DAHN-kruh

1589. Scanner.   Le scanner.   *luh SKAH-nehr*

1590. Power cord.   Un cordon.   *uhn kawr-DAWN*

1591. USB cable.   Un câble USB.   *un KAH-bluh ew-ehs-BAY*

1592. Monitor.   Un écran.   *uh nay-KRAHN*

1593. Mouse.   Une souris.   *ewn soo-REE*

1594. Mousepad.   Un tapis de souris.
uhn tah-PEE duh soo-REE

1595. Keyboard.   Un clavier.   *uhn klah-VYAY*

1596. Speakers.   Les enceintes.   *lay zahn-SEHNT*

1597. Headset.   Un casque.   *uhn kahsk*

1598. Webcam.   Une webcam.   *ewn WEHB-kahm*

1599. Flash drive.   Une clé USB.   *ewn klay ew-ehs-BAY*

1600. External hard drive.   Un disque dur externe.
uhn deesk dewr ehk-STEHRN

1601. MP3 player.   Un lecteur mp3.
uhn lehk-TUHR ehm-pay-TRWAH

1602. Hardware.   Le matériel.   *luh mah-tay-RYEHL*

1603. Software.   Le logiciel.   *luh law-zhee-SYEHL*

1604. Drivers.   Les pilotes.   *lay pee-LAWT*

1605. File.   Le dossier.   *luh DAW-syay*

1606. Attachment.   La pièce jointe.   *lah pee-ehs ZHWEHNT*

1607. Link.   Le lien.   *luh lyeh<u>n</u>*

1608. Search engine.   Le moteur de recherche.
luh maw-TUHR duh ruh-SHEHRSH

1609. Web browser.   Le navigateur.
luh nah-vee-gah-TUHR

1610. Internet user.   L'internaute.   *lehn-tehr-NOHT*

Keyboard Layouts

France

Belgium

Switzerland

French Canada

Canada (Multilingual Standard)

APPENDIX

Informal Language / *Le Langage Familier*

For the average tourist, understanding informal language is more important than attempting to use it in everyday conversations. The slang presented in this section should be considered for recognition purposes only. The vocabulary is listed in alphabetical order for quick reference, and the standard French equivalents are given in parentheses.

Nouns

Une bagnole (une voiture). Car; jalopy.

Des balles (euros, francs). Big ones.

Le bide (le ventre). Belly.

Un bordel (un désordre). Mess.

Une borne (un kilomètre). Kilometer.

La bouffe (la nourriture). Food.

Un boulot (un travail). Job.

Un bouquin (un livre). Book.

Une capote (un préservatif). Condom.

Un char (*Quebec*) (une voiture). Car.

Le cinoche (le cinéma). Movie theater.

Une clope (une cigarette). Cigarette.

Un costard (un costume). Suit.

Un fiston (un fils). Son.

Un flic (un agent de police). Cop.

La flotte (l'eau). Water.

Un frangin (un frère). Brother.

Une frangine (une sœur). Sister.

Le fric (l'argent). Money.

Les fringues (les vêtements). Clothes.

La galère (une situation difficile). Hassle, nightmare.

Un(e) gamin(e) (un enfant). Kid.

Une godasse (une chaussure). Shoe.

Un(e) gosse* (un enfant). Kid.

La gueule (le visage). Face.

Un mec (un homme). Guy.

Une nana (une femme). Woman.

Les people (les vedettes). Celebrities.

La piaule (une chambre). Bedroom.

Des piastres (Quebec) (dollars). Bucks.

Le pif (le nez). Nose.

Une pige (un an). Year.

Le pognon (l'argent). Money.

Un(e) pote (un copain/une copine). Pal, buddy.

Un rencard (un rendez-vous). Appointment; date.

---

* In Quebec, gosse means "testicle" and not "kid"!

Quick & to the Point

Terms of endearment / *Les mots de tendresse*

mon chou	my cabbage
ma biche	my doe
mon amour	my love
mon chéri / ma chérie	my darling
mon ange	my angel
ma puce	my flea
ma cocotte	my hen

La taule (la prison). Prison.

Le toubib (un médecin). Doctor.

Une toune (*Quebec*) (une chanson). Song.

Un tube (une chanson). Hit song.

Un type (un homme). Guy.

Les vieux (les parents). Parents

Adjectives / Adverbs

À sec (manque d'argent). Broke.

Barjo (fou). Crazy.

Bidon (faux). Fake.

Bourré (ivre). Drunk.

Carrément (très, même). Really, even.

Chiant (énervant). Annoying.

Cinglé (fou). Crazy.

Con (abruti / imbécile). Jerk / Idiot.

Crado (sale). Dirty.

Crevé (épuisé). Exhausted.

Débile (stupide). Stupid, idiotic.

Déjanté (excentrique). Oddball.

Dingue (fou). Crazy.

Feignant (paresseux). Lazy.

Fauché (manque d'argent). Broke.

Furax (furieux). Furious.

Futé (malin). Clever.

Godiche (maladroit, gêné). Awkward.

Gratos (gratuit). Free.

Kif-kif (même, pareil). All the same.

Loufoque (fou). Crazy.

Marrant (drôle). Funny.

Moche (laid). Ugly.

Niaiseux (Quebec) (stupide). Stupid.

Nickel (propre). Spotless.

Nunuche (stupide). Stupid.

Pas terrible (pas bon). Not good.

Platte (Quebec) (ennuyeux). Boring.

Radin (bon marché). Cheap.

Rigolo (drôle). Funny.

Ringard (démodé). Old-fashioned, out of style.

Roublard (malin). Cunning.

Salé (cher). Expensive (bill).

Timbré (fou). Crazy.

Vache (méchant). Mean.

Vachement (très). Really, very.

Verbs

Bosser (travailler). To work.

Bousiller (casser, bâcler). To break, wreck something.

Se casser (partir). To leave.

Causer (parler). To talk, chat.

Choper (attraper, voler). To get, catch, steal.

Engueuler (réprimander). To tell someone off.

Gerber (vomir). To throw up.

Gonfler (énerver). To annoy.

Larguer (abandonner, quitter). To abandon something; to dump someone.

Louper (rater, manquer). To miss; to mess up something.

Se marrer (rire). To laugh.

Mater (regarder). To look at.

Paumer (perdre). To lose.

Piger (comprendre). To understand.

Se planter (se tromper). To make a mistake.

Râler (se plaindre). To complain.

Rigoler (rire). To laugh.

Soûler (s'enivrer, énerver). To get drunk; to annoy someone.

Verlan

Verlan is a form of slang that reverses the syllables in words. The *Verlan* word is given first, and the original word from which it is derived follows in parentheses.

Chelou (louche). Shady, sketchy.

Féca (café). Coffee.

Keuf (flic). Cop.

Keum (mec). Guy.

Laisse béton (laisse tomber). Never mind.

Meuf (femme). Woman.

Ouam (moi). Me.

Ouat (toi). You.

Poteca (capote). Condom.

Reuch (cher). Expensive.

Reuf (frère). Brother.

Reum (mère). Mother.

Reup (père). Father.

Teuf (fête). Party.

Vénère (énervé). Annoyed.

Expressions

C'est du gâteau!
It's a piece of cake!

Revenons à nos moutons.
Let's get back to the subject.

Ça saute aux yeux.
That's obvious.

C'est dans la poche.
It's a sure thing.

Ça ne tourne pas rond.
Something's wrong.

C'est pas sorcier.
It's not rocket science.

Je vais jeter un œil.
I'll take a look.

Ça n'a rien à voir avec . . .
That has nothing to do with . . .

Ça vaut le coup.
It's worth it.

Ç'est parti!
Here we go / we're off!

Oh purée!
Oh my goodness!

Ça fait un bail!
It's been a long time!

Ça craint! / C'est nul!
That sucks!

Je m'en fiche!
I don't care!

À un de ces quatre!
See you one of these days!

J'ai la pêche!
I feel great!

Tu vas tomber dans les pommes?
Are you going to pass out?

Il va péter les plombs.
He's going to go crazy.

J'en reviens pas!
I can't believe it!

J'en ai marre! / Je suis tanné(e)! (*Quebec*)
I'm fed up!

On voit que dalle.
We can't see anything.

Quand les poules auront les dents!
When pigs fly!

Occupe-toi de tes oignons!
Mind your own business!

Ce n'est pas la mer à boire.
It's not the end of the world.

J'ai d'autres chats à fouetter.
I have other fish to fry.

Interjections

Aïe! / Ouïe! / Ouille! Ouch!

Beurk! Berk! Yuck!

Bof! Whatever!

Boum! Boom! Bang!

Chiche! I dare you! Go ahead!

Chut! Shush! Be quiet!

Et après? Who cares?

Hein? Huh?

Gla gla! Brrrrrrr!

Hop-là! Whoopsie-daisy!

La vache! Rats!

Merde! Damn! / Break a leg! (to an actor)

Miam miam! Yum yum!

Mince! Darn! Dang it!

Ouf! Phew!

Ouste! Scram!

Pan! Bang!

Toc, toc! Knock knock!

Vlan! Slam!

Youpi! Yay!

Zut! Darn!

Abbreviations

Un accro (accroché). Addict.

Un ado (adolescent). Teenager.

Bon Anniv' / Annif' (Bon anniversaire). Happy Birthday.

Un apéro (apéritif). Before-dinner drink.

Un appart (appartement). Apartment.

Un aprem (après-midi). Afternoon.

Bon app (Bon appétit). Have a good meal.

Un car (autocar). Bus.

Comme d'hab (Comme d'habitude). As usual.

Un dico (dictionnaire). Dictionary.

Extra (extraordinaire). Great.

La fac (faculté). University.

Le foot (football). Soccer.

Impecc (impeccable). Perfect, spotless.

Un imper (imperméable). Raincoat.

Intello (intellectual). Intellectual.

MacDo (McDonald's). McDonald's.

Une manif (manifestation). Protest demonstration.

Swear words / Les jurons

Swear words that show anger or dissatisfaction (such as *damn* in English) are quite different between Europe and Quebec. In Europe, you may hear words such as **purée**, **flûte**, **zut**, or **mince**, whereas in Quebec, **calvaire**, **viarge**, and **maudit** are common.

Vulgar words (comparable to four-letter words in English) that should not be used in polite company also differ between the two continents. In Europe, **fait chier**, **merde**, **putain** and **putain de merde** are considered more offensive. In Quebec, the more offensive words include **câlice**, **ostie** and **tabernak.**

Un ordi (ordinateur). Computer.

P'ti déj' (petit déjeuner). Breakfast.

Le proprio (propriétaire). Landlord.

Sympa (sympathique). Nice, cool, great.

La télé (télévision). Television.

Public Holidays / Les Jours Fériés

Most shops, as well as banks and post offices, are closed on Sundays and public holidays, and public transportation is reduced.

France

January 1	**Jour de l'An**	New Year's Day
Monday after Easter	**Lundi de Pâques**	Easter Monday
May 1	**Fête du Travail**	Labor Day
May 8	**Victoire 1945**	Victory in Europe Day
6th Thursday after Easter	**Ascension**	Ascension
Monday after Pentecost	**Lundi de Pentecôte**	Whit Monday
July 14	**Fête Nationale**	National Holiday
August 15	**Assomption**	Assumption of Mary
November 1	**Toussaint**	All Saint's Day
November 11	**Armistice 1918**	End of World War I
December 25	**Noël**	Christmas Day

Belgium

January 1	**Jour de l'An**	New Year's Day
Monday after Easter	**Lundi de Pâques**	Easter Monday
May 1	**Fête du Travail**	Labor Day
May 8	**Victoire 1945**	Victory in Europe Day
6th Thursday after Easter	**Ascension**	Ascension

Monday after Pentecost	**Lundi de Pentecôte**	Whit Monday
July 21	**Fête Nationale**	National Holiday
August 15	**Assomption**	Assumption of Mary
November 1	**Toussaint**	All Saint's Day
November 11	**Armistice 1918**	End of World War I
December 25	**Noël**	Christmas Day

Quebec

January 1	**Jour de l'An**	New Year's Day
Friday before Easter	**Vendredi saint**	Good Friday
Monday after Easter	**Lundi de Pâques**	Easter Monday
Monday preceding May 25	**Journée nationale des Patriotes**	National Patriot's Day
June 24	**Fête nationale** (*Québec*)	National Holiday
July 1	**Fête nationale** (*Canada*)	National Holiday
First Monday in September	**Fête du Travail**	Labor Day
Second Monday in October	**Fête de l'Action de grâce**	Thanksgiving
December 25 and 26	**Noël et l'Après-Noël**	Christmas

Switzerland

Each canton in Switzerland decides on its public holidays, with the exception of the *Fête Nationale* on August 1.

		FR	GE	JU	NE	VS	VD
January 1	New Year's Day	x	x	x	x	x	x
January 2	St. Berchtold	x		x	x		x
March 1	Republic Day				x		
March 19	St. Joseph's Day					x	
varies	Good Friday	x	x	x	x		x
varies	Easter Monday	x	x	x	x		x
May 1	Labor Day	x	x				
varies	Ascension	x	x	x	x	x	x
varies	Whit Monday	x	x	x	x		x
varies	Corpus Christi	x		x		x	
August 1	National Holiday	x	x	x	x	x	x
August 15	Assumption	x		x		x	
November 1	All Saint's Day	x		x		x	
December 8	Immaculate Conception	x				x	
December 25	Christmas Day	x	x	x	x	x	x
December 26	St. Stephen's Day	x					

FR: Fribourg   GE: Genève   JU: Jura
NE: Neuchâtel   VS: Valais   VD: Vaud

Famous Sites

Paris

L'Arc de Triomphe. *lark duh tree-AWNF*

La Bibliothèque Nationale. *lah bee-blee-aw-TEHK nah-syaw-NAHL*

Le Bois de Boulogne. *luh bwah duh boo-LAWN-yuh*

Le Bois de Vincennes. *luh bwah duh vehn-SEHNN*

La Cimetière de Père-Lachaise. *lah seem-TYEHR duh pehr-lah-SHEHZ*

Le Centre Georges Pompidou. *luh SAHN-truh zhohrzh pawn-pee-DOO*

Les Champs-Élysées. *lay shahn-zay-lee-ZAY*

Les Halles. *lay ahl*

L'Hôtel des Invalides. *loh-TEHL day zehn-vah-LEED*

Île de la Cité. *eel duh lah see-TAY*

La Grande Arche de la Défense. *lah grahnd ahrsh duh lah day-FAHNS*

Le Louvre. *luh LOO-vruh*

Montparnasse. *mawn-pahr-NAHSS*

Montmartre. *mawn-MAHR-truh*

Le Musée de Cluny. *luh mew-ZAY duh klew-NEE*

Le Musée d'Orsay. *luh mew-ZAY dawr-SAY*

Notre-Dame. *naw-truh DAHM*

L'Opéra. *loh-pay-RAH*

Le Palais de Justice. *luh pah-LEH duh zhews-TEESS*

Le Palais du Luxembourg. *luh pah-LEH dew lewk-sahn-BOOR*

Le Palais-Royal. *luh pah-LEH rwah-YAHL*

Le Panthéon. *luh pahn-tay-AWN*

La Place de la Concorde. *lah plahss duh lah kawn-KAWRD*

La Place Vendôme. *lah plahss vahn-DOHM*

Les Quais. *lay kay*

Le Quartier Latin. *luh kahr-tyay lah-TEHN*

Sacré-Cœur. *sah-kray-KUHR*

La Sainte-Chapelle. *lah SEHNT-shah-PEHLL*

La Salle Luxembourg. *la sahl lewk-sahn-BOOR*

La Sorbonne. *la sawr-BAWNN*

Le Théâtre français. *luh tay-AH-truh frahn-SEH*

La Tour Eiffel. *lah toor ay-FEHL*

Les Tuileries. *lay tweel-REE*

Brussels

L'Arc de Triomphe. *lark duh tree-AWNF*

Atomium. *ah-toh-mee-UHM*

Le Centre Belge de la Bande Dessinée. *luh SAHN-truh behlzh duh lah bahnd day-see-NAY*

Coudenberg. *koo-dahn-BEHRG*

La Grand-Place. *lah grahn PLAHSS*

Manneken Pis. *MAHNN-uh-kuhn PEESS*

Le Musée Horta. *luh mew-ZAY ohr-TAH*

Le Parc du Cinquantenaire. *luh pahrk dew sehn-kahn-tuh-NEHR*

Le Palais Royal. *luh pah-LEH rwah-YAHL*

La Place du Grand Sablon. *la plahss dew grahn sah-BLAWN*

Geneva

La Cathédrale Saint-Pierre. *lah kah-tay-DRAHL sehn-PYEHR*

L' Horloge fleurie. *lawr-LAWZH fluh-REE*

Le Jet d'eau. *luh zheh DOH*

Le Mur des Réformateurs. *luh MEWR day RAY-fawr-mah-TUHR*

L'Office des Nations unies. *law-FEES day nah-SYAWN zew-NEE*

Le Parc des Bastions. *luh pahrk day bahs-TYAWN*

Le Parc des Eaux Vives. *luh pahrk day ZOH-VEEV*

Le Palais des Nations. *luh pah-LEH day nah-SYAWN*

La Place du Bourg-de-Four. *la plahss dew boorg-dew-FOOR*

La Place Neuve. *lah plahss NUHV*

La Rade de Genève. *lah rahd duh zhuh-NEHV*

APPENDIX

Quebec City and Montreal

Le Biodôme de Montréal. *luh BEE-oh-DAWM duh mawn-ray-AHL*

Le Chateau Frontenac. *luh shah-TOH frawn-tuh-NAHK*

La Citadelle de Québec. *lah see-tah-DEHL duh kay-BEHK*

La Chute Montmorency. *lah SHEWT mawn-moh-rahn-SEE*

Le Jardin Botanique de Montréal. *luh zhahr-DEHN baw-tah-NEEK duh mawn-ray-AHL*

Les Jardins de Métis. *lay zhahr-dehn duh may-TEESS*

Le Marché Bonsecours. *luh mahr-SHAY bawn-suh-KOOR*

Le Musée de l'Amérique française. *luh mew-ZAY duh lah-may-REEK frahn-SEHZ*

L'Observatoire de la Capitale. *lawb-zehr-vah-TWAHR duh lah kah-pee-TAHL*

Le Parc Jean-Drapeau. *luh pahrk ZHAHN-drah-POH*

Le Parc Maisonneuve. *luh pahrk MEH-zaw-NUHV*

Le Parc du Mont-Royal. *luh pahrk dew mawn-rwah-YAHL*

La Place-Royale. *lah plahss rwah-YAHL*

Le Plateau. *luh plah-TOH*

Geographical Names in Frequent Use

Where the French spelling differs, it is given in parentheses after the English.

Annecy. *ahn-SEE*

Antibes. *ahn-TEEB*

Antwerp (Anvers). *ahn-VEHR*

Arles. *arl*

Avignon. *ah-veen-YAWN*

Basel (Bâle). *bahl*

Basque. *bahsk*

Biarritz. *bee-ah-REETS*

Bordeaux. *bawr-DOH*

Boulogne. *boo-LAWN-yuh*

Brittany (Bretagne). *bruh-TAHN-yuh*

Brussels (Bruxelles). *brewk-SEHL*

Burgundy (Bourgogne). *boor-GAW-nyuh*

Caen. *kahn*

Calais. *ka-LEH*

Cannes. *kahnn*

Chambéry. *shahn-bay-REE*

Chamonix. *shah-maw-NEE*

Chenonceaux. *shuh-nawn-SOH*

Chartres. *SHAHR-truh*

Cherbourg. *shehr-BOOR*

Corsica (Corse). *kawrss*

Côte d'Azur. *koht da-ZEWR*

Flanders (Flandre). *FLAHN-druh*

Fontainebleau. *fohn-tehn-BLOH*

167

Gatineau. *gah-tee-NOH*

Geneva (Genève). *zhuh-NEHV*

Lausanne. *loh-ZAHNN*

Laval. *lah-VAL*

Le Havre. *luh AHV-ruh*

Liège. *lyehzh*

Lille. *leel*

Loire. *lwahr*

Luxembourg. *LEWK-sahn-BOOR*

Lyons (Lyon). *lee-AWN*

Marseilles (Marseille). *mar-SAY-uh*

Meuse. *muhz*

Mons. *mawnss*

Mont Saint-Michel. *mawn sehn-mee-SHEHL*

Montreal (Montréal). *mawn-ray-AHL*

Nantes. *nahnt*

Neuchâtel. *NUH-shah-TEHL*

Nice. *neess*

Normandy (Normandie). *nawr-mahn-DEE*

Paris. *pa-REE*

Provence. *praw-VAHNSS*

Québec. *kay-BEHK*

Reims. *rehnss*

Rhône. *rohnn*

Rouen. *roo-ah<u>n</u>*

Saint-Cloud. *seh<u>n</u> CLOO*

Saint-Laurent. *seh<u>n</u> loh-RAH<u>N</u>*

Saint-Malo. *seh<u>n</u> mah-LOH*

Sainte-Foy. *seh<u>n</u>t-FWAH*

Savoy (Savoie). *sah-VWAH*

Seine. *sehnn*

Sept-Îles. *seht-EEL*

Strasbourg. *strahz-BOOR*

Touraine. *too-REHNN*

Tours. *toor*

Trois-Rivières. *trwah-ree-VYEHR*

Versailles. *vehr-SAH-yuh*

Wallonia (Wallonie). *wah-law-NEE*

Driving in Europe

Foreign tourists (at least 21 years old) may rent a car and drive in Europe with a regular driver's license. However, automatic cars are somewhat rare and more expensive to rent, plus they generally run on gasoline instead of diesel, which is also more expensive. If you cannot drive a manual transmission, be sure to reserve an automatic well in advance.

Driving in Europe can be radically different from driving in North America. The major differences include no right turn at a red light, left lanes on the highway are used for passing only, in addition to the numerous roundabouts and "priorité à droite" in France.

Priorité à droite (priority to the right) applies when you approach an intersection and there is either no sign to indicate who has the priority or a *priorité à droite* sign (a triangle with a red outline and a black X in the middle).

You must yield to traffic coming from the right, unless your road is marked with the priority road sign (a yellow diamond inside a white diamond).

The majority of roundabouts in France do not use *priorité à droite,* with the exception of *La Place Étoile* in Paris and roundabouts that are under construction and have no other signs posted. Therefore the priority goes to cars already in the roundabout, and those entering need to yield.

For the standard roundabout with four roads, you need to be in the right lane if you intend to turn right or go straight through the roundabout. If you intend to turn left or turn around and go back the way you came from, you need to be in the left lane. When entering a roundabout, you should turn your left blinker on until you get close to the road where you will be turning, then switch to your right blinker when you are ready to turn.

Within city limits, the speed is limited to 50 kph, and outside of city limits, it is 90 kph. When entering a new city or town, you will see the name on a white sign with a red outline. This is the signal to decrease your speed. When leaving, you will see the name with a red line through it. This is the signal that you may increase your speed.

On highways, the speed limit is 130 kph, unless it is raining, snowing, or foggy, in which case the speed is limited to 110 kph.

 Highways in France are not free, and there are frequent tollbooths (*péages*). Many require you to take a ticket first and pay when you exit, but some do require payment first. The automatic machines at the tollbooths do not take American credit cards, so you must make sure to enter the lanes marked with the green arrow so that you can give cash (coins or bills) to the person in the tollbooth. Occasionally there will be automatic tollbooths that accept coins, but it is somewhat rare for bills.

In Belgium, the main differences from France are a speed limit of 120 kph on the highways and the absence of tolls.

In Switzerland, the speed limit on highways is also 120 kph, and even though there are no tollbooths, a vignette sticker must be bought (40 CHF or 25€) and placed on the windshield in order to drive on the highways. This vignette may be bought at the border when entering Switzerland.

In Luxembourg, the speed limit is 130 kph as in France, but similar to Belgium, there are no tolls.

In France and Luxembourg, the signs indicating highways are blue and the signs indicating national roads are green.

 In Belgium and Switzerland, the colors are the opposite. Highways are marked in green and national roads are blue.

Driving in Canada is not much different from driving in the United States, with the exception of right turn on red. This is illegal on the island of Montréal, but legal everywhere else in Canada. Highway speeds in Quebec are limited to 100 kph in rural areas and 70-90 kph in urban areas. Highway speeds tend to be slightly higher (110 kph) in other parts of Canada.

Road Signs and Public Notices / Les Panneaux de Signalisation et les Avis

Aller.
al-LAY
Go

Allumez vos feux.
ah-lew-MAY voh fuh
Turn on headlights.

Arrêtez.
ar-reh-TAY
Stop.

Attention.
ah-tah<u>n</u>-SYAW<u>N</u>
Drive carefully.

Avertissez.
ah-vehr-tee-SAY
Honk horn.

Boulevard.
bool-VAR
Boulevard.

Carrefour.
kar-FOOR
Intersection.

Cassis.
ka-SEE
Dip.

Cédez le passage.
say-day luh pah-SAHZH
Yield.

Croisement.
krwahz-MAH<u>N</u>
Crossroads.

Danger.
dah<u>n</u>-ZHAY
Danger.

Défense de doubler.
day-FAH<u>N</u>S duh doo-BLAY
No passing.

Défense d'entrer.
day-FAHNS dahn-TRAY
Keep out.

Défense de fumer.
day-FAHNS duh few-MAY
No smoking.

Deuxième vitesse.
duh-ZYEHM vee-TEHSS
Use second gear.

Déviation.
day-vee-ah-SYAWN
Detour.

École.
ay-KAWL
School.

Entrée.
ahn-TRAY
Entrance.

Fermée.
fehr-MAY
Closed.

Fils à haute tension.
feel ah oht tahn-SYAWN
High-tension lines.

Lentement.
lahn-tuh-MAHN
Slow.

Passage à niveau.
pah-SAHZH ah nee-VOH
Railroad crossing.

Péage.
pay-AHZH
Tollbooth.

Pente dangereuse.
pahnt dahn-zhuh-RUHZ
Steep grade.

Pont étroit (provisoire).
pawn ay-TRWAH (praw-vee-ZWAHR)
Narrow (temporary) bridge.

Priorité à droite.
pree-aw-ree-TAY ah DRWAHT
Give way to the right.

Ralentissez.
rah-lahn-tee-SAY
Slow down.

Roulez au pas.
roo-lay oh PAH
Drive slowly.

Route étroite.
roo tay-TRWAHT
Narrow road.

Route sinueuse.
root SEE-new-UHZ
Winding road.

Sens unique.
sahn sew-NEEK
One way.

Sortie.
sawr-TEE
Exit.

Stationnement.
stah-syawnn-MAHN
Parking.

Stationnement interdit.
stah-syawnn-MAHN ehn-tehr-DEE
No parking.

Tenez à droite.
tuh-NAY za drwaht
Keep right.

Tournant.
toor-NAHN
Curve.

Tournant double.
toor-NAHN DOO-bluh
Double curve.

Travaux.
tra-VOH
Construction.

Virage.
vee-RAHZH
Sharp turn.

Virage à droite (gauche) interdit.
vee-RAHZH ah drwaht (gohsh) eh̲n-tehr-DEE
No right (left) turn.

Vitesse maximum ____ kilomètres à l'heure.
vee-TEHS max-ee-MUHM ____ kee-law-MEH-trah LUHR
Maximum speed ____ kilometers per hour.

FRENCH FOOD AND WINE SUPPLEMENT

A visit to France can be your introduction to the imagination, spirit, and tradition of the French cuisine. France is very rich in natural resources and all these resources have been used creatively. In less abundant regions, dishes are prepared using foods and ingredients that are relatively unknown and unpopular in North America. Ingredients are extensive, seasonings are subtle, and regional resources are developed to the utmost. French dining is not only enhanced by the art of cooking, but also by the complementary art of serving. There is a pride and joy in cooking and serving—whether it be of a simple or complex nature—that is at once noticeable. To understand the spirit and tradition of French cooking and dining is to begin to understand the spirit of the French people.

Breakfast in France is quite simple. It has come to be known as the continental breakfast; but in France more accurately *café complet* consists of freshly baked *croissants, brioches,* or French bread served with butter and jelly and *café au lait,* that is, coffee with hot milk. Lunch, usually served between 12 and 2 o'clock, is frequently the main meal of

177

the day. It is a leisurely meal and carefully planned. Dinner is customarily served between 7 and 9 o'clock and is as significant as the midday meal. Wines are, of course, served with all meals; whether it be an ordinary table wine or a carefully chosen vintage wine, drinking wine is considered a natural complement for the full enjoyment of food.

The list that follows is by no means complete but is meant to serve as an introduction to the tourist to what may at first appear to be a bewildering French menu. Dishes are alphabetized according to the French and usually appear as they would on a French menu. Descriptions are necessarily brief and have been written for the purpose of rapid reference.

Note on Hors d'Œuvres

The preparation and serving of hors d'œuvres can be quite simple or very elaborate, but it remains an essential part of French cuisine. The custom of serving cold or hot hors d'œuvres for lunch and dinner is traditional on all French menus. Interesting and imaginative combinations of fish, shellfish, salad, eggs, vegetables, meats, and marinated dishes are usually included and served in small tasteful combinations. We have not included a list of the extensive hors d'œuvres possible for the purpose of this "Native Food List." Listed simply as HORS D'ŒUVRES on the menu, this course varies daily with the spirit of the chef, and the quality of the restaurant you choose to dine in. It is usually an adventure in the tradition of French dining.

Useful Menu Terms

L'addition / La note. The check.

À la carte or **carte.** A list of individual dishes at a fixed price.

À prix fixe. At a fixed price.

Carte du jour. Menu or bill of fare.

Menu. Fixed-price meal (starter + main dish + dessert).

Formule. Restricted fixed-price meal (starter + main dish or main dish + dessert).

Couvert. Cover charge.

Déjeuner. Lunch.

Dîner. Dinner.

Petit déjeuner. Breakfast.

Inclusif. Included.

Plat. A single course or dish.

Selon grosseur or **S.G.** According to size.

Service compris. Service charge included.

Sommelier. Wine steward.

Spécialités. Specialties.

Supplément. Additional charge.

Sur commande. On special order.

Table d'hôte. The house lunch or dinner at a fixed price.

Styles of Preparation: Some General Terms

À la . . . In the style of ___

À l'andalouse. Served with green peppers and tomatoes.

À l'africaine. Served with rice.

À l'anglaise. Boiled.

À l'aubergiste. Prepared in the customary style of the restaurant or inn.

À l'autrichienne. Austrian style; seasoned with paprika and caraway seeds.

À la grecque. Greek style with olive oil.

À la minute. Quickly prepared.

À la mode. . . In the style of ___

À la russe. With sour cream.

À point. Used to describe the preparation of meat as medium or done to a turn.

Assorti. Assorted.

Au gratin. Baked in a cream sauce with a garnish of cheese and bread crumbs.

Au jus. With natural juice of the beef.

Au kirsch. Mixed with the brandy, kirsch. Usually refers to fresh fruit.

Au lait. With milk.

Au maigre. Meatless dish.

Au vin rouge. Prepared with red wine.

FOOD AND WINE SUPPLEMENT

Bellevue. Served in aspic accompanied by a white sauce garnished with truffles, tongue, and tarragon.

Bien cuit. Well done.

Blanchi. Blanched.

Bouilli. Boiled.

Bourgeoisie. Cooked in hearty family style with carrots, onions, potatoes, and bacon.

Braisé. Braised.

Brochette. Meat or fish and vegetables grilled on a skewer over the open fire.

Brouillé. Scrambled.

Canapé. Small, daintily prepared open sandwich served as an appetizer.

Casserole. Food served in an individual dish.

Charolais. Charcoal broiled.

Châtelaine. Garnish of artichoke hearts, tomatoes, and small roast potatoes.

Chiffonade. Served with shredded vegetables.

Cocotte. Served in an individual earthenware or copper pot.

Confiserie. Sweets and candies.

Croûton. Diced toast fried in butter or oil and used for soups, salads, and garnish.

Désossé. Boneless.

Diable. Deviled. Prepared in highly seasoned style.

FOOD AND WINE SUPPLEMENT

Dolmas. Chopped liver or other meat and vegetables wrapped in vine leaves, cabbage leaves, or peppers.

Émincé. Minced meat dish served with a seasoned sauce.

En papillote. Baked in an oiled paper bag to allow steaming in natural juices.

Entremets. Additional course after the roast.

Escalope. Thinly sliced meat.

Étuvé. Stewed.

Farci. Stuffed.

Flambé. Served flaming in rum or brandy.

Frit. Fried.

Galantine. Rolled or pressed meat or poultry prepared with stock and gelatine and served cold. Usually a buffet or lunch dish.

Gelé. Jellied.

Glacé. Iced.

Gratiné. Served with bread crumbs or cheese.

Grillade. A grilled dish.

Grillé. Grilled or broiled.

Haché. Chopped or sliced.

Hachis. Hash.

Hongroise. Hungarian style; prepared with sour cream and paprika.

Indienne. Curried.

Jardinière. Fresh vegetables attractively cut and used as a garnish.

Julienne. Cut in thin strips.

Lyonnaise. Served with onions.

Macédoine. Combination of cut-up fruits or vegetables.

Macéré. Pickled.

Nature or **au naturel.** Plain, uncooked.

Panaché. Mixed.

Pané. Prepared with bread crumbs.

Parmentier. Prepared with potatoes.

Pâté. Creamy paste made with fish, poultry, or meat and distinctively seasoned.

Paysanne. Country style; a regional preparation.

Printanière. Garnished with diced spring vegetables.

Provençale. Prepared with oil, vinegar, herbs, garlic. Served hot or cold.

Purée. Mashed or strained.

Quenelle. Oval shaped balls made with chopped chicken, veal, or fish and seasonings.

Ragoût. Stew.

Rissoles or **rissolettes.** Minced meat fried in a thin pastry.

Rochambeau. Garnish of carrots, lettuce, and cauliflower.

Saignant. Medium rare.

Saumuré. Pickled or marinated.

Sauré. Cured in smoke.

Sauté. Gently browned in butter.

Timbale. Traditional French mold for baking and preparing hot or cold desserts.

Véronique. Garnished with grapes.

Viande fumée. Smoked meat.

Sauces and Condiments

Allemande. White sauce made with veal stock, egg yolk, lemon juice and seasonings.

Anchois. Anchovy sauce.

Aurore. Chicken and tomato sauce.

Béarnaise. Subtly seasoned sauce made with butter, shallots, egg yolks, tarragon, and wine.

Béchamel. Thick, creamy white sauce.

Bercy. Sauce made with fish stock, wine, and shallots.

Beurre blanc. White butter sauce.

Beurre fondu. Melted butter sauce.

Beurre noir. Browned butter with vinegar and parsley.

Beurre roux. Browned butter sauce.

Bigarrade. Duck stock, orange and lemon juice and rind combined in a sauce for duckling.

Bolognaise. Spicy sauce prepared with garlic, tomatoes, vegetables, and seasonings.

Bonne femme. Rich, creamy sauce.

Bordelaise. Wine sauce made with stock, seasonings, shallots, and wine.

Bourguignonne. Wine sauce made with onions, spices, beef stock, and red wine.

Bretonne. Fish sauce made with fish stock, leeks, celery, beans, and mushrooms.

Câpre. Caper sauce made with fish stock, butter, and capers; served with fish.

Cardinal. Béchamel sauce and red lobster butter.

Chasseur. Butter or olive oil, mushrooms, tomato sauce, and meat glaze combined with white wine and brandy.

Créole. Sauce made with onions, tomatoes, and peppers for rice.

Diable. Hot, spicy sauce made with wine, vinegar, fresh pepper, and shallots.

Duglère. Rich, creamy sauce made with fish stock, butter, eggs, cream, wine, and tomatoes.

Espagnol. Rich, brown sauce made with meat stock, vegetables, and tomatoes.

Fines herbes. Sauce made with finely chopped herbs; usually served with fish, fowl, and omelettes.

Gastronome. White wine sauce.

Génoise. Cold sauce made with mayonnaise, cream, and nuts.

FOOD AND WINE SUPPLEMENT

Hollandaise. Rich, creamy sauce made with egg yolks, butter, and lemon juice; usually served with fish or vegetables.

Indienne. Curry sauce.

Journeaux. Chicken liver sauce.

Livornaise. Sauce of anchovy paste, oil, and eggs.

Madère. Madeira wine sauce.

Maître d'hôtel. Light sauce made with butter, lemon juice, and parsley.

Marguery. White wine sauce for fish and seafood.

Matelote. Sauce of fish stock, wine, mushrooms and anchovies; usually served with fish.

Meunière. Butter sauce.

Mornay. Rich cream sauce garnished with grated cheese.

Mousseline. Creamy hollandaise sauce.

Moutarde. Mustard.

Nantus. Sauce made with crayfish, white wine, vegetables, and tomatoes.

Newburg. Rich sauce combining sherry, cream, egg yolks, and lobster meat.

Niçoise. Sauce made with onions, garlic, oil, tomatoes, and vegetables; used for fish, chicken, or meat.

Normande. Cream sauce combined with fish stock and mushrooms.

Périgueux. Sauce made with stock, wine, tomatoes, and truffles.

Périgourdine. Rich madeira wine sauce made with truffles and goose livers.

Piquante. Spicy sauce.

Poivrade. Highly seasoned sauce made with freshly ground peppercorns, onions, and stock.

Portugaise. Tomato and vegetable sauce.

Printanière. White sauce with green vegetables and parsley.

Raifort. Horseradish.

Ravigote. Sauce made with wine, vinegar, stock, shallots, and fresh tarragon; served hot or cold.

Régence. White wine sauce with mushrooms and truffles.

Rouennaise. Red wine sauce made with duck livers, bay leaves, and thyme; usually served with duck.

Robert. Spicy meat sauce made with onions, wine, meat stock or glaze, mustard, and sugar.

Sabayon. Rich, frothy dessert sauce made with marsala wine, eggs, sugar whipped together and flavored to taste.

Saupiquet. Spiced vinegar sauce.

Soubise. Béchamel sauce with finely minced onions.

Smitane. Sour cream sauce with sautéed onions and white wine.

Suprême. Rich sweet cream sauce.

Tartare. Cold, well-seasoned sauce made with mayonnaise, vinegar, mustard, pickles, herbs; usually served cold.

Verte. Mayonnaise seasoned and colored with green vegetables.

Velouté. Rich, creamy sauce for chicken or fish.

Vinaigrette. Sauce or a dressing for vegetables or salads made with oil, vinegar, mustard, and spices.

Breads and Butters

Brioche. Light, sweet, breakfast roll.

Croissant. Flaky, crescent-shaped breakfast roll.

Pain. Bread.

Pain grillé. Toast

Pain noir. Wheat or rye bread.

Pain perdu. French toast.

Petit pain. Roll.

Beurre. Butter.

Beurre d'anchois. Anchovy butter.

Soups

Bisque. Rich, creamy soup made with a basic fish stock, fish, or shellfish.

Bisque d'écrevisses. Crayfish soup.

Bisque de homard. Lobster soup.

Bisque d'huîtres. Oyster soup.

Bouillabaisse. Hearty fish soup, much like stew, made with a variety of fish, wine, tomatoes, onion, garlic, saffron, fennel and served with French bread.

Bouillabaisse à la marseillaise. Bouillabaisse prepared with Mediterranean fish.

Bouillon. Broth.

Consommé. Clear broth made with chicken or meat and vegetables and served with various garnishes.

Consommé brunoise. Clear beef soup.

Consommé vert. Green consommé made with asparagus tips, peas, string beans, sorrel leaves, and chervil.

Crème d'asperges. Cream of asparagus soup.

Crème de carottes. Cream of carrot soup.

Crème de champignons. Cream of mushroom soup.

Crème d'épinards. Cream of spinach soup.

Crème Olga. Mushroom and onion soup.

Crème vichyssoise. Cold, piquant soup made with potatoes and leeks.

Marmite or **petite marmite.** Classic French soup prepared with beef, poultry, and vegetables. Traditionally served in an earthenware pot with toasted bread and cheese.

Potage. Soup.

Potage à l'ail. Garlic soup served with cheese.

Potage bonne femme. Leek and potato soup.

Potage bourguignonne. Hearty vegetable and meat soup.

FOOD AND WINE SUPPLEMENT

Potage cressonnière. Purée of potato and watercress soup.

Potage grand duc. Cauliflower soup.

Potage du jour. Particular soup prepared for the day.

Potage au lentilles. Lentil soup.

Potage Marguerite. Kidney bean soup.

Potage à la milanaise. Vegetable and meat soup with cheese.

Potage parmentier. Potato soup.

Potage portugais. Spicy tomato soup.

Potage à la reine. Cream of chicken soup.

Potage au vermicelle. Noodle soup.

Potage de volaille. Chicken broth.

Pot-au-feu. Traditional hearty soup similar to **petite marmite**.

Poule au pot. Chicken and broth served in the pot.

Soupe au chou. Cabbage soup.

Soupe aux moules. Mussel soup.

Soupe à l'oignon. Onion soup served with toasted bread and cheese.

Soupe aux poissons. Fish soup.

Vichyssoise. Potato and leek soup made with sour cream; served cold.

Fish and Shellfish

Aigrefin. Haddock.

Arachon. French oyster.

Banquet. Prawn.

Bar de mer. Sea bass.

Blanchaille. Whitebait.

Brème. Bream (a fish in the carp family).

Brochet badoise. Baked pike prepared with sour cream.

Cabillaud au four. Baked codfish.

Carpe à la polonaise. Carp cooked in red wine with onions and almonds.

Carrelet. Flounder.

Caviar frais. Fresh caviar.

Chaudfroid de saumon. Cold salmon in jellied sauce.

Clovisse. Clam.

Coquillages. Shellfish.

Coquilles provençale. Scallops in a dried mushroom sauce.

Coquilles St. Jacques. Baked scallops au gratin.

Cotriade. Fish stew.

Crevettes. Shrimp.

Croustade aux langoustes. Pastry shell filled with creamed lobster.

Darne. Slice of fish with the bone.

FOOD AND WINE SUPPLEMENT

Darne Montmorency. Slice of salmon with mushrooms and olives.

Écrevisse. Crayfish.

Escargots. Snails.

Escargots à la bourguignonne. Snails cooked in wine sauce and baked in well-seasoned butter.

Esturgeon. Sturgeon.

Féra. Whitefish.

Filet de sole amandine. Fillet of sole sautéed in butter sauce and garnished with shredded almonds.

Filet de sole bonne femme. Sole prepared in a white wine sauce and hollandaise sauce.

Filet de sole dieppoise. Sole prepared in a sauce of mussels and shrimp.

Filet de sole aux huîtres. Fillet of sole poached, sautéed in butter and prepared with oysters.

Filet de sole mâconnaise. Sole in red wine sauce.

Filet de sole à la Mornay. Fillet of sole with a cheese sauce.

Flet. Flounder.

Flétan. Halibut.

Fruits de mer. Seafood.

Hareng. Herring.

Hareng fumé. Smoked herring.

Hareng mariné. Marinated herring.

Hareng salé. Kipper.

Hareng saur. Red herring.

Homard. Lobster.

Homard à l'américaine *or* **armoricaine.** Lobster meat in a rich tasty sauce of butter, stock, fresh tomatoes, wine, and brandy.

Homard en bellevue *or* **aspic de homard en bellevue.** Lobster in fish aspic.

Homard à la Newburg. Lobster Newburg (lobster meat in a sherry cream sauce).

Homard Marguerite. Lobster with mushrooms and truffles in a rich cream sauce with wine.

Homard parisienne. Cold, boiled lobster served in the shell with mayonnaise dressing.

Homard thermidor. Lobster thermidor (lobster meat mixed with rich cream sauce and wine; baked in the shell, covered with cheese and bread crumbs).

Huîtres en cheval. Oysters on horseback (oysters rolled in bacon, grilled, and served on toasted bread squares).

Huîtres en coquille. Oysters on the half shell.

Laitance. Fish roe.

Langouste. Crawfish or crayfish (European lobster similar to American varieties).

Langoustines. Prawns (a large kind of shrimp).

Loup. Bass.

FOOD AND WINE SUPPLEMENT

Maquereau mariné. Marinated mackerel.

Marennes. Small oysters.

Matelote. Fish stew.

Médaillons de poissons. Halibut steaks.

Merlan. Whiting.

Merluche. Dried codfish.

Morue provençale. Codfish in tomato sauce.

Moules. Mussels.

Moules bordelaise. Mussels in wine sauce.

Moules farcies. Stuffed mussels.

Moules marinière. Mussels steamed in a wine sauce with butter and shallots.

Moules panées. Baked mussels.

Moules à la provençale. Mussels cooked in a spicy sauce made with oil, garlic, wine, fish stock, and herbs.

Œufs de poisson. Fish roe.

Palourde. Clam.

Panchouse. Fish stew made from fresh-water fish.

Perche. Perch.

Pieuvre. Octopus.

Plie. Plaice (similar to sole).

Pochouse bourguignonne. Fish stew.

Poireaux aux crevettes. Shrimp with leeks.

Poisson. Fish.

Poulpe. Octopus.

Quenelles de brochet. Fish or meat dumplings.

Raie au beurre noir. Sea skate sautéed in brown butter.

Rouget au fenouil. Mediterranean fish cooked in olive oil with bacon and seasoned with fennel.

Rousette. Variety of salmon.

Royan. Herring.

Salmis de poissons. Mixed seafood.

Sardines à l'huile. Sardines in olive oil.

Sardines à la niçoise. Sardines cooked in a white wine sauce with mushrooms and spices.

Saumon fumé. Smoked salmon.

Saumon glacé or **chaudefroid de saumon.** Cold salmon in aspic.

Saumonneau. Baby salmon.

Scampi. Large shrimp prepared in seasoned garlic sauce.

Sole Albert. Sole with oysters and mushrooms.

Sole arlésienne. Sole cooked with garlic, onions, tomatoes and spices.

Sole Colbert. Boned fillet of sole, breaded and fried.

Sole gratin. Sole baked with bread crumbs, mushrooms and cheese.

Sole limande. Lemon sole.

Sole Margeury. Sole prepared with a rich cream sauce of shrimp, mushrooms, and wine.

Sole Mirabeau. Sole with anchovy sauce.

Sole Olga. Sole poached and stuffed into baked potatoes and garnished with a rich shrimp sauce.

Sole Orly. Sole fried in deep fat and served with tomato sauce.

Sole vin blanc. Sole in a cream sauce made with wine, stock, egg yolks, and cream.

Tacaud. Variety of codfish.

Tanche. Variety of carp.

Thon à l'huile. Tuna fish in oil.

Truite. Trout.

Truite au bleu. Fresh trout poached in water and vinegar resulting in a bluish color.

Truite saumonée. Salmon trout.

Turbatin. Native French fish similar to flounder.

Turbot. Fish similar to flounder.

Turbot bonne femme. Turbot cooked in cream sauce with wine, mushrooms, and shallots.

Turbot au champagne. Turbot poached in white wine or champagne.

Vandoise. Variety of carp.

Vangeren. Variety of carp.

Entrees: Meats and Miscellaneous Dishes

Bifteck tartare. Raw chopped beef usually served with an accompanying sauce.

Blanquette d'agneau. Lamb stew with mushrooms and onions.

Blanquette de veau. Veal stew in a rich sauce.

Bœuf à la mode. Marinated beef braised with carrots, mushrooms, and onions.

Bœuf bouilli. Boiled beef.

Bœuf bourguignonne. Beef stew with red wine, tomato paste, onions, and mushrooms.

Bœuf en daube. Beef stew with red wine.

Bœuf salé. Corned beef.

Carbonnade. Beef prepared in the oven with onions, beer, and beef stock.

Carbonnade à la flamande. Browned slices of beef cooked in seasoned beer sauce.

Carré de porc rôti. Roast loin of pork.

Cassoulet. Native stew made with white beans, sausage, pork, tomatoes (sauce or paste), onions, garlic, and bacon rind, cooked and served in casserole.

Cervelles au beurre noir. Calves' brains served with browned butter.

Cervelles beurre noisette. Poached brains in hazelnut-butter sauce.

FOOD AND WINE SUPPLEMENT

Châteaubriand. Thick steak cut from middle of the beef fillet.

Choucroute garni. Hot sauerkraut served with a variety of meats and sausages.

Cochon de lait. Suckling pig.

Côte de veau. Veal cutlet.

Côtelette de veau en papillote. Veal cutlet baked and served in a sealed paper container.

Côtes de bœuf. Ribs of beef.

Côtes de porc. Spareribs.

Cuisseau. Leg of veal.

Daube. Stew usually made with lamb or mutton, herbs, vegetables, and wine.

Entrecôte. Thin rib steak.

Entrecôte chasseur. Steak served with a wine sauce.

Entrecôte château. Large, thick steak.

Entrecôte minute. Very thin slice of beef steak for quick broiling.

Épaule de veau. Shoulder of veal.

Escalopes de veau panées. Thinly sliced veal, lightly breaded and fried and garnished with lemon and chopped egg.

Escalopes de veau à la royale. Sliced veal in brandied cream sauce.

Estouffade. Braised beef with wine, stock, onions, garlic, herbs, and mushrooms.

Estouffade de bœuf. Beef stew with red wine and onions.

Estouffade de haricots. Stew of sausage, pork, and white beans.

Filet de bœuf. Fillet of beef; one of the choicest cuts.

Filet mignon. Choice of fillet of beef.

Filet de porc. Pork fillet.

Filets de veau. Veal fillets.

Foie à la bordelaise. Liver with wine and mushrooms.

Foie gras. Finely ground goose liver mixed with chicken forcemeat, truffles, salt, pepper, and brandy. Served hot or cold as a delicacy.

Foie à la provençale. Liver sautéed in garlic butter.

Foie de veau. Calf's liver.

Foie de veau moissonnière. Calf's liver with onions, herbs, and red wine.

Foie de volaille. Chicken liver.

Fricadelles. Meat patties made with chopped beef, onions, and seasoning.

Fricandeau. Sliced meat in wine sauce.

Fricassée de veau. Veal stew.

Gigot d'agneau. Leg of lamb.

Gigot de mouton. Leg of mutton.

FOOD AND WINE SUPPLEMENT

Goulasch de veau. Veal goulash.

Grenouilles sautées fines herbes. Frog's legs sautéed in butter with finely chopped herbs and lemon.

Haricots de mouton. Mutton stew with beans, onions, and carrots.

Jambon. Ham.

Jambon à la crème. Ham in cream sauce.

Jambon au madère. Ham in madeira wine sauce.

Langue de bœuf. Ox tongue.

Langue de veau. Calf's tongue.

Navarin de mouton. Mutton stew.

Noisettes d'agneau. Boneless lamb chops.

Paupiette. Large slice of meat, rolled and stuffed with forcemeat and baked.

Paupiette de veau. Slice of veal, stuffed and rolled.

Petit salé. Salt or pork bacon.

Pied de veau. Calf's feet grilled or baked.

Plat de côtes au chou. Boiled beef and cabbage.

Poitrine de veau. Breast of veal.

Pot-au-feu. Boiled beef with vegetables; served in the pot.

Potée limousine. Stew of pork, cabbage, and chestnuts.

Pré salé. Lamb fed in salt marshes causing its distinctive taste; a regional specialty of Normandy.

Quenelles. Dumpling stuffed with a tasty preparation of minced meat or fish.

Queue de bœuf. Oxtail.

Quiche Lorraine. Open-baked pie filled with a mixture of chopped ham or bacon, beaten eggs, cream, and cheese.

Ragoût d'agneau. Lamb stew.

Ragoût de bœuf. Beef stew.

Ragoût de mouton jardinière. Mutton stew with finely cut carrots, turnips, onions, potatoes, and peas.

Ris d'agneau. Lamb sweetbreads.

Ris de veau. Veal sweetbreads.

Rognons de mouton. Sheep kidneys.

Saucisse. Fresh pork sausage.

Saucisson. Smoked pork sausage.

Sauté de bœuf. Beef sautéed in a wine and tomato sauce.

Selle d'agneau. Saddle of lamb.

Selle de veau. Saddle of veal.

Steak à l'américaine. Grilled steak served with a fried egg.

Steak de cheval. Horsemeat steak.

Steak Diane. Very thin steak.

Steak haché. Chopped steak.

Steak au poivre. Choice cut of steak covered with freshly crushed peppercorns and melted butter, then broiled.

Tendrons de veau. Braised veal.

Terrine maison. Finely ground mixture of chicken goose liver, pork, and distinctive seasonings; very often a regional specialty.

Tournedos. Center cut of beef or a small thick fillet, sautéed or grilled and garnished in many different ways.

Tournedos à la béarnaise. Grilled fillet of beef served with béarnaise sauce.

Tournedos chasseur. Beef fillet cooked in butter and garnished with a sauce of mushrooms, tomatoes, and wine.

Tournedos Rossini. Grilled fillet of beef garnished with goose liver, truffles, and a wine sauce.

Tranche de bœuf. Slice of steak.

Tripe à la mode. Tripe cooked with tomatoes, shallots, and apple brandy.

Veau. Veal.

Veau Marengo. Sliced veal sautéed in olive oil with wine, mushrooms, and tomatoes.

Veau mimosa. Veal with port wine and fresh tarragon.

Poultry and Game

Aguillettes de caneton. Breast of duckling.

Ailerons de poulet. Chicken wings.

Bécasse. Woodcock.

Bécassine. Snipe.

Brochettes de foies de volaille. Skewer of chicken livers brushed with butter and grilled on an open flame.

Cailles. Quails.

Canard. Duck.

Canard Montmorency. Duck cooked in a rich sauce made with whole bing cherries.

Canard aux olives. Duck prepared in a sauce with olives.

Canard à la presse. Pressed duck served in flaming brandy.

Canard sauvage. Wild duck.

Caneton. Duckling.

Caneton aux cerises. Duckling with cherries.

Caneton à l'orange. Duckling with orange sauce.

Caneton aux pommes. Roast duckling with apples.

Caneton rouennais. Duckling served with a rich sauce made with duck stock, cognac, red wine, and onions.

Caneton sauvage. Wild duckling.

Chapon. Capon (castrated rooster).

Civet de lièvre à la française. Hare cooked in a red wine sauce with mushrooms and onions.

Civette. Hare stew.

Coq à la bourguignonne. Rooster simmered with wine, brandy, onions, and mushrooms.

Coq au vin. Chicken cooked in wine, brandy, onions, and mushrooms.

FOOD AND WINE SUPPLEMENT

Côtelettes de poulet. Chicken cutlets.

Cou d'oie farci. Stuffed goose neck.

Crêpes niçoises. Pancake stuffed with a tasty chicken preparation.

Crochettes de volaille. Chicken croquettes.

Croustade de volaille. Pastry shells filled with well-seasoned minced chicken.

Dinde. Turkey.

Dindonneau. Young turkey.

Faisan. Pheasant.

Filets de poulets. Breasts of chicken.

Foies de volaille et rognons au vin rouge. Chicken livers and kidneys sautéed in red wine.

Fricassée de poulet. Chicken fricassee.

Galantine de volaille. Chicken served in a decorative mold; made with chicken stock and gelatin.

Ganga. Species of grouse.

Gelinotte. Hazel hen (a game bird).

Grand coq de bruyère. Grouse.

Grive. Thrush.

Lapereau. Young rabbit.

Lapin. Rabbit.

Lapin chasseur. Rabbit stew with wine, tomatoes, mushrooms, and herbs.

Lièvre. Hare.

Lièvre à la royale. Hare stew made with wine, vinegar, carrots, onions, and garlic.

Marcassin. Young boar.

Merles. Blackbirds; usually roasted.

Oie or **oison.** Goose.

Ortolans. Small delicate birds; prepared as a table delicacy.

Pain de volaille froid. Cold chicken loaf.

Pâté d'alouettes. Lark pie.

Pâté de cailles. Quail pie.

Pâté de poulet. Pâté of chicken made with chicken, truffles, brandy, seasoning, forcemeat, and enclosed in puff pastry and baked.

Perdreau. Partridge.

Perdrix. Partridge.

Pigeonneaux or **pigeons.** Squab.

Poularde. A hen or fat pullet especially fattened for the kitchen.

Poularde en brioche. Chicken baked in yeast dough.

Poularde en chemise. Poached, stuffed chicken.

Poularde à l'estragon. Chicken prepared with fresh tarragon.

Poularde de grain. Spring chicken.

Poularde lyonnaise. Stuffed chicken cooked with truffles and vegetables.

Poularde Marengo. Chicken dish made with olive oil, wine, stock, fresh tomatoes or tomato paste, and black olives.

Poularde à la Périgord. Chicken stuffed with truffles and baked in a glazed sauce.

Poularde au riz. Well-seasoned chicken garnished with rice.

Poularde strasbourgeoise. Chicken breasts stuffed with pâté de foie gras.

Poularde à la tartare. Chicken brushed with olive oil and bread crumbs, usually served with sauce.

Poularde en terrine à la gelée. Chicken stuffed with force-meat, prepared in an aspic and usually served on ice for hors d'œuvres or cold buffet.

Poularde vin blanc. Chicken with white wine.

Poule au pot. Chicken in the pot.

Poulet. Young chicken.

Poulet amandine. Chicken cooked in a wine sauce with tomatoes, stock, sour cream, and garnished with shredded almonds.

Poulet armagnac. Chicken cooked in a sauce with Armagnac brandy.

Poulet bourguignonne. Chicken cooked in a red wine with onions and mushrooms.

Poulet chasseur. Chicken sautéed in olive oil, butter, shallots, and tomato sauce.

Poulet à la crème. Chicken in a rich cream sauce.

Poulet dinde. Baby turkey.

Poulet de grain en casserole. Spring chicken cooked and served in a casserole; usually in a wine sauce with onions, carrots, turnips, celery, leeks, and mushrooms.

Poulet de grain grillé diable. Broiled deviled spring chicken; sautéed in butter, brushed with mustard, bread crumbs.

Poulet grillé. Grilled chicken.

Poulet à la Kiev. Boned chicken breasts, stuffed with a finger of sweet butter and fried.

Poulet à la king. Chicken à la king; sautéed chicken served in a cream sauce with mushrooms and grated cheese.

Poulet Marengo. Chicken sautéed in olive oil with wine, mushrooms, stock, tomatoes, and olives.

Poulet niçoise. Chicken cooked with garlic, saffron, and tomatoes.

Poulet paysanne. Chicken with vegetables.

Poulet sauté. Chicken lightly cooked in butter.

Poulet sauté aux fines herbes. Sautéed chicken seasoned with parsley, chevril, and tarragon.

Poulet sauté indienne. Curried chicken.

Poulet sauté à la Maintenon. Sautéed chicken with mushrooms.

Poulet sauté provençale. Chicken sautéed in olive oil and simmered in a well-seasoned wine sauce with herbs.

Poulet à la Stanley. Chicken with mushrooms and paprika.

Poussin. Very young chicken.

Quenelle de volaille. Chicken dumpling.

Salade de poulet. Chicken salad.

Salmis. Birds or game birds stewed in wine.

Sanglier. Boar.

Selle de chevreuil. Saddle of roebuck; usually served with a sauce.

Soufflé de volaille. Chicken soufflé.

Suprêmes de poulet. Breasts of chicken.

Suprêmes de volaille aux champignons. Sautéed chicken breasts served with mushrooms in a delicately seasoned sauce with varied garnishes.

Suprêmes de volaille parisienne. Sautéed chicken cooked in a wine sauce and served with a rich mushroom sauce or hollandaise.

Venado. Venison.

Vol-au-vent. Light puff pastry filled with chicken or meat in a rich, cream sauce.

Omelets

Omelette aux artichauts. Omelet with artichoke hearts.

Omelette au lard. Omelet with bacon.

Omelette bonne femme. Bacon and onion omelet.

Omelette célestine. Jam omelet.

Omelette aux cèpes. Sliced mushroom omelet.

Omelette aux champignons. Mushroom omelet.

Omelette au confiture. Jam omelet.

Omelette aux crevettes. Shrimp omelet.

Omelette espagnole. Spanish omelet.

Omelette aux fines herbes. Omelet with finely chopped herbs.

Omelette foies de volaille. Omelet with sautéed chicken livers.

Omelette au fromage. Cheese omelet.

Omelette au jambon. Ham omelet.

Omelette au lard. Bacon omelet.

Omelette à la lyonnaise. Omelet with finely minced sautéed onions.

Omelette nature. Plain omelet.

Omelette aux oignons. Chopped onion omelet.

Omelette Parmentier. Diced potato omelet.

Omelette aux pommes de terre. Potato omelet.

Omelette provençale. Omelet made with onions, garlic, and tomatoes.

Omelette aux rognons. Kidney omelet.

Omelette à la Rossini. Omelet made with foie gras and truffles.

Omelette soufflée. Light, puffed omelet; usually a lunch or dessert dish.

Omelette aux tomates. Tomato omelet.

Potatoes

Pommes de terre allemande. Cooked potatoes, sliced and fried in butter.

Pommes de terre allumettes. Fried shoe-string potatoes.

Pommes de terre Alphonse. Cooked potatoes, sliced and mixed with diced sweet peppers, brushed with maître d'hôtel butter (butter with parsley and dash of lemon juice), and baked with grated cheese.

Pommes de terre à l'anglaise. Peeled boiled potatoes.

Pommes de terre Anna. Sliced potatoes baked and browned in butter in the oven.

Pommes de terre bouillée. Boiled potatoes.

Pommes de terre boulangère. Quartered potatoes baked with minced, sautéed onions.

Pommes de terre "chip." Thin, crisp fried potato chips.

Pommes de terre à la crème. Creamed potatoes.

Pommes de terre dauphine. Sliced potatoes baked with butter and grilled Swiss cheese.

Pommes de terre duchesse. Boiled potatoes, mashed with egg yolks and butter, shaped into patties and fried or baked.

Pommes de terre farcies. Stuffed potatoes.

Pommes de terre au four. Baked potatoes.

Pommes de terre frites. French fried potatoes.

Pommes de terre hongroise. Sliced potatoes with onion, paprika, moistened with bouillion and baked.

Pommes de terre au lard. Potatoes fried with bacon.

Pommes de terre Lorette. Mashed potatoes mixed with eggs and butter, shaped into crescents and deep fat fried.

Pommes de terre lyonnaise. Cooked, sliced potatoes sautéed with sliced onions.

Pommes de terre Macaire. Baked potatoes mashed and prepared in pancake style and browned in an omelet pan of hot butter.

Pommes de terre maître d'hôtel. Sliced potatoes cooked in milk and served with chopped parsley.

Pommes de terre marquise. Cooked potatoes with tomato purée shaped into patties and sautéed in butter.

Pommes de terre mousseline. Cooked mashed potatoes with cream; shaped and glazed.

Pommes de terre nouvelles. New potatoes.

Pommes de terre à la parisienne. Potato balls rolled in a meat glaze and sprinkled with parsley.

Pommes de terre Parmentier. Sautéed diced potatoes.

Pommes de terre persillées. Boiled potatoes rolled in melted butter and parsley.

Pommes de terre en purée. Mashed potatoes.

Pommes de terre rissolées. Roast potatoes.

Pommes de terre en robe des champs. Potatoes baked in the jacket.

Pommes de terre sautées. Sautéed potatoes.

Pommes de terre soufflées. Very light whipped potatoes.

Pommes de terre surprise. Baked, stuffed potatoes.

Vegetables and Vegetable Dishes

Rice and Noodle Dishes

Abbatis au riz. Giblets with rice.

Artichauts à la grecque. Artichokes cooked in herbs and olive oil; usually served cold.

Asperges au gratin. Asparagus in a rich creamy cheese sauce and buttered bread crumbs.

Asperges vinaigrette. Asparagus with oil and vinegar.

Aubergine. Eggplant.

Aubergine farcie. Stuffed, baked eggplant.

Carottes flamandes. Creamed carrots.

Carottes glacées. Glazed carrots.

Carottes râpées. Grated carrots.

Céleri braisé. Braised celery.

Céleri rave. Celery root served as a hot vegetable or a cold hors d'œuvre in a piquant sauce.

Cèpes à la moelle. Mushrooms cooked with pieces of marrow.

Cèpes provençale. Wild meaty mushrooms (bolitus variety) prepared with onions, garlic, tomatoes.

Champignons. Small mushrooms.

Champignons farcis. Stuffed mushrooms.

Champignons grillés. Mushrooms grilled in butter.

Chanterelles. Type of mushroom.

Chou-au-lard. Cabbage cooked with bacon.

Choucroute garnie. Hot sauerkraut with meat and sausage.

Chou-fleur à l'huile. Cauliflower marinated in oil and vinegar; served cold.

Chou de Bruxelles. Brussels sprouts.

Choux farcis. Stuffed cabbage.

Cœur de céleri. Hearts of celery.

Concombre. Cucumber.

Coquillettes. Elbow macaroni.

Courgettes niçoises. Squash with onions and rice.

Endive au jus. Sautéed endive.

Endive au meunière. Endive baked in butter.

Épinards en branche. Spinach cooked in butter.

Épinards à la crème. Creamed spinach.

Flageolets. Small kidney beans.

Fond d'artichauts. Hearts of artichokes.

Girolle. Variety of mushroom.

Haricots rouges au vin. Red beans cooked in wine.

Haricots verts sautés. Sautéed string beans.

Laitue paysanne. Lettuce cooked with ham, onions, and carrots.

Laitue de printemps braisée au bacon. Braised lettuce with bacon.

Légumes panachés. Mixed vegetables.

Macaroni au fromage. Macaroni with cheese.

Macaroni au gratin. Macaroni with Béchamel sauce, sprinkled with grated cheese and melted butter, and baked.

Macaroni à la Nantua. Cooked macaroni mixed with crayfish, baked and served in a timbale or mold.

Macédoine de légumes. Mixture of diced, fresh vegetables.

Nouilles au fromage. Noodles and cheese.

Petits pois à la française. Tiny peas cooked with butter, finely minced onion and lettuce.

Petits pois au jambon. Peas with minced onion and ham.

Petits pois aux laitues. Peas with lettuce.

Points d'asperges. Tender, green asparagus tips.

Pois à la française. Green peas cooked with onions and lettuce.

Purée de légumes. Creamed preparation of finely chopped vegetables.

Purée St. Germain. Creamed green peas.

Purée soubise. Creamed onions.

Ratatouille. Chopped eggplant, green peppers, tomatoes, onions, garlic, and olive oil; a dish of Arabic origin.

Risotto à la turque. Rice with saffron and tomatoes.

Riz à la créole. Rice with tomatoes and pimentos.

Riz à la grecque. Cooked rice with chopped onion, peas, sweet red pepper, and shredded lettuce.

Riz sauvage. Wild rice.

Riz à la valencienne. Rice, tomatoes, saffron, onion, and shellfish.

Tomates farcies. Stuffed tomatoes.

Tomates grillées. Grilled whole tomatoes.

Tomates sautées à la provençale. Seasoned sliced tomatoes sautéed in olive oil with garlic, garnished with parsley and bread crumbs, and baked.

Truffes. Type of fungus that thrives underground, considered a true delicacy. Can be used as an hors d'œuvre or vegetable but more usually a garnish.

Truffes au champagne. Truffles in champagne sauce; served in pastry crust.

Truffes à la crème. Truffles in rich cream sauce and brandy; served in light pastry crust.

Salads

French salads are varied but quite simple in preparation. Dressings are added in small quantities and garlic is used very sparingly; perhaps the secret of French salad excellence is that it is mixed just before serving.

Salade de betterave. Thinly sliced beet salad with finely chopped herbs.

Salade caprice. Similar to a chef's salad: various kinds of lettuce with a julienne of tongue, ham, chicken, and artichoke hearts.

Salade de céleri. Hearts of celery.

Salade de chèvre chaud. Green salad topped with goat's cheese melted on toasted baguette slices.

Salade de chicorée aux tomates. Chicory and tomato salad.

Salade de chou rouge. Red cabbage salad.

Salade de chou. Coleslaw.

Salade de concombres. Thinly sliced cucumbers with oil, vinegar, and chervil.

Salade de cresson. Watercress salad.

Salade cressonnière. Salad mixture of potatoes, watercress, parsley, chervil, and hard-boiled egg.

Salade d'haricots secs et de lentilles. Haricot beans and lentil salad with thinly sliced onion.

Salade d'haricots verts. String bean salad.

Salade italienne. Assortment of raw or cooked vegetables with salami, anchovies, olives, and capers with a mayonnaise dressing.

Salade de laitue et betteraves. Lettuce and beet root salad.

Salade de légumes. Freshly cooked vegetable salad with oil and vinegar dressing.

Salade de lentilles. Salad of cold boiled lentils, well seasoned.

Salade niçoise. Salad of string beans, diced potatoes, tomatoes, olives, anchovies, and hard-boiled eggs served with oil and vinegar.

Salade panachée au cresson. Mixed salad with watercress.

Salade de pissenlit. Dandelion salad.

Salade de poireau. Leek salad.

Salade de pommes de terre. Potato salad.

Salade de romaine à l'estragon. Salad of romaine lettuce with fresh tarragon.

Salade russe. Mixture of cooked vegetables, ham, lobster; all cut julienne style and mixed with mayonnaise.

Salade de saison. Salad of the season.

Salade de scarole aux fines herbes. Escarole salad with finely chopped herbs.

Salade de tomates. Sliced tomatoes served in a tasty mixture of oil, vinegar, and herbs.

Salade verte. Mixed green salad.

Saladier. Salad bowl.

Cheese

Beaufort de Savoie. Similar to Swiss gruyère; made of cow's milk.

Bonvillois. Soft, creamy white cheese.

Brie. Round, flat, creamy white cheese; made with cow's milk.

Cabrion. Goat's milk cheese.

Cachat. Cheese made with ewe's milk in Provence.

Camembert. Creamy, ripe cheese; made with cow's milk in Normandy.

Cantal. Small, hard cheese; made in Auvergne.

Chabris. Goat's milk cheese.

Chèvre. Chèvreton. Chevrotin. Chevrotton. Goat's milk cheese; made in many varieties, sizes and shapes.

Coulommiers. Creamy, sharp cow's milk cheese; from the Île de France region.

Crème Chantilly. Creamy, mild dessert cheese.

Demi-sel. Light cream cheese made with cow's milk.

Dreux. Soft-textured cheese made with cow's milk.

Emmental. Gruyère cheese with holes; from Emme valley in Switzerland.

Fontainebleau. Cream cheese.

Forez. Similar to Roquefort cheese.

Fromage blanc. Cottage cheese.

Fromage à la crème. Cream cheese.

Fromage de chèvre. Goat's milk cheese.

Fromage de Hollande. Dutch cheese; usually refers to Edam.

Géromé. Sharp cheese made with cow's milk.

Marlieu. Round, mild, white cheese.

Maroilles. Cow's milk cheese, with a pungent smell, made in northern France.

Neufchâtel. Mild, creamy cheese from Normandy.

Olivet. Soft cheese from Orléans.

Persillé. Similar to Roquefort.

Petit suisse. Cream cheese.

Pont-l'Évêque. Semi-hard cheese from Normandy.

Port-du-Salut or **Port-Salut.** Soft, smooth cheese with distinctive flavor.

Providence. Similar to Port-du-Salut.

Reblochon. Soft whole milk cheese; from the Loire Valley.

Roquefort. Sharp, pungent, blue-veined cheese made with ewe's milk, and well-aged.

Septmoncel. Hard cheese similar to Roquefort.

Suisse. Swiss cheese.

Tomme de Savoie. Cheese produced from skim milk in the Alps.

Trouville. Similar to Pont-l'Évêque.

Vendôme. Similar to Camembert.

Desserts

Africains. Small dessert cookies.

Ananas au kirsch. Pineapple steeped in kirsch brandy.

Assiette de friandises. Assortment of fancy cookies.

Baba au rhum. Light yeast cake soaked in rum.

Beignet. Doughnut; usually with a jelly filling.

Biscuits. Biscuits or delicate cookies usually served with ice cream.

Bombe. Mold of ice cream, whipped cream, and fruit; or several flavors of ice cream combined.

Bugne. Type of doughnut.

Brownie. Brownie.

Café liégeois / viennois. Coffee ice cream with whipped cream.

Cerises jubilée. Brandied cherries served aflame over ice cream.

Chantilly. Whipped cream.

Charlotte Malakoff. Rich, creamy dessert made with lady fingers, whipped cream, and almonds.

Compôte. Stewed fruit in light syrup.

Cookie. Cookie.

Cornet de glace. Ice cream cone.

Corbeille de fruits. Basket of fruit.

Coupe favorite. Ice cream flavored with kirsch, garnished with whipped cream and strawberry purée.

Coupe glacée. Ice cream topped with whipped cream; similar to the American sundae.

Coupe (St.) Jacques. Ices or ice cream heaped with diced fresh fruit in kirsch.

Crème caramel. Light caramel cream pudding.

Crème Chantilly. Whipped cream with sugar.

Crème dessert. Pudding.

Crêpes au sucre. Thin pancakes served with sugar.

Crêpes Suzette. Thin pancakes steeped in a sauce made with butter, sugar, oranges, liqueurs, and brandy, flamed in a chafing dish.

Crumble. Crumble.

Dartois. Cake made of light puff pastry usually filled with pastry cream or jelly.

Diplomate. Cold pudding made with crushed fruit and whipped cream.

FOOD AND WINE SUPPLEMENT

Doigt de dame. Meringue lady fingers.

Éclair. Éclair filled with whipped cream or custard.

Éclair au café. Coffee éclair.

Éclair au chocolat. Chocolate éclair.

Fraises à la crème. Fresh strawberries served with sugar and cream.

Fraises des bois. Small very fresh wild strawberries.

Fraises Romanoff. Strawberries steeped in orange juice and curaçao with ice cream or whipped cream.

Framboises. Fresh wild raspberries.

Fruits frais. Fresh fruit.

Galette bretonne. Round, flat, tasty cookie made in Brittany.

Gâteau. Cake; **Gâteau de maison** is the cake specialty of the house.

Gâteau d'amande. Almond cake.

Génoise. Smooth-textured yellow cake used for **petits fours** and sponge rolls.

Glace. Ice cream or ices.

Glace à la vanille. Vanilla ice cream.

Glace au chocolat. Chocolate ice cream.

Glace aux fraises. Strawberry ice cream.

Glace aux fruits. Ice cream with crushed fruit or fruit syrup.

Glace napolitaine. Combination of ices and ice cream.

Glace panachée. Mixed ice cream.

Granité. Ices with fruit syrup.

Liégeois. Soft ice cream dessert.

Macédoine de fruits. Mixture of fresh fruits and liqueur.

Madeleine. Small butter cookie.

Marignan. Sponge cake filled with whipped cream.

Marquise. Ices with whipped cream.

Marrons glacés. Candied chestnuts.

Massepain. Marzipan (colorful and decorative candy-like cookies made with almonds, sugar, eggs, and flavoring).

Mazarin. Yeast cake with kirsch brandy and sabayon sauce.

Melba. Dessert sauce made with raspberries, currant jelly, lemon juice, and sugar.

Melon glacé. Cold melon.

Melon frappé. Iced melon with liqueur.

Meringue. Confection of egg whites and sugar.

Meringue glacée. Ice cream in a swirl of baked egg whites.

Mille-feuille. Flaky puff pastry used as a tart or for cookies.

Mirabelles. Small yellow plums.

Moka. Pastry with mocha cream frosting.

Mont Blanc. Fruit or chestnut purée with flavored whipped cream.

Mousse. Light sweet dessert made with whipped cream and lightly beaten eggs.

Mousse au chocolat. Chocolate mousse.

Mousse de fraises. Strawberry mousse.

Napoléon. Whipped cream or light custard sandwiched between flaky layers of delicate pastry.

Nesselrode. Sauce or tart filling made with brandied fruits and chestnuts in a rich syrup.

Nougat. Confection of almonds, pistachio nuts, honey, and sugar.

Omelette flambée au rhum. Omelet served with flamed rum sauce and powdered sugar.

Parfait. Any combination of ice cream, whipped cream, and fruits served in a tall glass.

Pâtisserie. General term for pastry.

Pêche Melba. Vanilla ice cream with peaches and crushed raspberry syrup.

Petit sablé. Cookie.

Petits fours. Small cakes or cookies.

Petits pots de crème. Cold custard dessert prepared in many different flavors and served in small traditional French crocks.

Poire cardinal. Stewed pears with raspberry sauce and toasted almonds.

Poire Hélène. Stewed pears with vanilla ice cream and chocolate sauce.

Pomme au beurre. Baked apple.

Pomme bonne femme. Baked apple.

Pot au crème. Custard dessert served in traditional crock.

Pouding. Pudding.

Profiterole. Small, flaky pastry filled with custard, ice cream, or whipped cream; usually served with chocolate sauce.

Pudding de cabinet. Pudding made with candied fruits, raisins, liqueur, and lady fingers.

Pudding de riz. Rice pudding.

Pudding soufflé. Light, fluffy pudding made with stiffly beaten egg whites.

Riz impératrice. Rice pudding with candied fruit and whipped cream; served cold.

Sablés. Small, tasty cookies.

Savarin. Rum-soaked sponge cake served with fruit and garnished with whipped cream.

Sorbet. Sherbet.

Soufflé. Egg yolks, stiffly beaten whites, and an extensive variety of fruit, flavors, and syrup are the basic ingredients for a favorite dessert or entrée. Served cold or hot and sometimes flamed.

Soufflé au chocolat. Chocolate soufflé.

Soufflé aux liqueurs. Soufflé flavored distinctively with a particular liqueur.

FOOD AND WINE SUPPLEMENT

Soufflé à la vanille. Vanilla soufflé.

Stanislas. Cake with almond cream filling.

Tarte. Open pastry shell filled with fruit or custard.

Tarte aux fraises. Strawberry tart.

Tartelettes. Little tarts filled with fruit or custard.

Tranche napolitaine. Ice cream slice of several flavors.

Tranche plombières. Ice cream with fruit.

Vacherin. Merinque shell filled with whipped cream.

Yaourt. Yogurt.

A Note on French Wines

France is renowned for producing a great variety of wines and for producing wines of a good quality. Viticulture is an ancient and respected art in France and French wine growers are concerned with maintaining the quality of their product. The authenticity and quality of the wine is also guaranteed by the laws, known as *Appellation Contrôlée* or *Appellation d'Origine,* which regulate the entire process of wine production in most areas of the country. These laws ensure that the wine label accurately identifies the contents of the bottle.

The wine laws governing the production of wine in a specific vineyard are stricter than the laws controlling the production of wine in larger areas. Therefore, a wine label that indicates a specific vineyard or origin suggests a wine of higher quality than a label that denotes only a region or a district of origin. This is why the first-quality, famous

French wines are always bottled under the name of a specific vineyard.

When you are traveling throughout France, do not feel that you should drink only the great wines. Most of these wines are readily available in the United States, whereas many delightful local wines are not. The local wines will be pleasant, inexpensive, and unique, and will add to the pleasures of dining in France.

"Wine rules" are the result of much loving experimentation by food and wine connoisseurs and are not meant to be social dictates. One should feel free to experiment, but the time-honored "rules" are often helpful.

An elementary rule-of-thumb concerning the serving of wine with food is that red wines complement red meats and white and rosé wines complement fish, shellfish, chicken, and the lighter meats, such as veal. Champagne is considered an excellent dinner wine and goes well with almost any dish.

General Suggestions for Selecting Dinner Wines

With	Try
Chicken Fish Shellfish Light meats (veal)	Dry white wine or rosé. Chablis is particularly good with oysters.
Red meats Game Cheese	Full-bodied red wines, i.e. Burgundy, Bordeaux, or Rhône.
Turkey	Dry red or white wine.

Sweet dessert	Sweet white wine, e.g., Sauternes or
Fruit	Barsac. Extra-dry champagne is also
	good.

Wine List

Apéritifs

It is customary in France to take a leisurely *apéritif* (an alcoholic wine drink), rather than a strong cocktail, to stimulate the appetite before the dinner. Popular apéritifs are:

Byrrh. Medium-dry, ruby red wine with body and subtle flavor.

Campari. Very dry, rather bitter white wine from Italy.

Dubonnet. Rich red, slightly sweet wine.

Pastis. Licorice root and anise-flavored liqueur, diluted with water before serving.

Pernod. Pale green liqueur with a distinctive anisette flavor. Served with water and ice.

Sherry. Amber-colored wine from Spain. Dry, light varieties are best served before dinner or with dinner.

Vermouth. Red (sweet) or white (dry) wine interestingly flavored with aromatic herbs and bitters. Usually served on ice with a twist of lemon peel.

Vermouth-cassis. Vermouth and cassis (a sirupy liqueur made from black currants) in a pleasant tasting mixture with ice and vichy water.

Red and White Table Wines

Alsatian wines. White wines similar to Rhine wines, produced in three different types.

>**Riesling.** Dry white wine.

>**Traminer.** Medium-dry wine with a pronounced spicy or fruit flavor and renowned bouquet.

>**Sylvaner.** Mild, pleasant white wine.

Barsac. Sweet, rich white wine of delicate aroma. Generally used as a dessert wine.

Bordeaux. Also referred to as claret. Red wines comparable in quality to Burgundy, but drier and lighter with elegant bouquet and flavor. The following districts produce excellent claret:

>**Saint-Emilion.** Full-bodied and robust wines with strong bouquet.

>**Pomerol.** Somewhat lighter wines, but otherwise similar to Saint-Emilion.

>**Médoc.** Typical claret. Light-bodied, mellow with long-lasting taste.

Burgundy. Full-bodied dry wine of excellent color, flavor, and strong bouquet. Produced in both red and white varieties. Some popular and generally available Burgundies are:

>**Nuits-Saint-Georges.** Red, very full-bodied with remarkable bouquet.

>**Pommard.** Somewhat light and more delicate.

Beaujolais. Fresh, light red Burgundy with an earthy bouquet. Excellent when drunk young.

Chablis. Very dry, light white wine with a peculiar "steely" flavor.

Champagne. The best sparkling wine in the world, produced in white and pink varieties. Champagne is made in varying degrees of sweetness and types:

Brut. Very dry.

Extra Sec. Semi-dry.

Sec. Less dry, actually rather sweet.

Blanc de blancs. Extremely light and effervescent.

Rhône. Full-bodied red wines of strong bouquet. Popular varieties are:

Côte-Rôtie.

Châteauneuf-du-Pape.

Rosé. Light, refreshing pink wines which are excellent when drunk young. The most popular rosé wines are:

Tavel. Dry, rather tart, highly praised wine.

Provence. Light, fresh and fruity wine.

Sauternes. Sweet, rich white wine. Generally used as a dessert wine.

Brandies, Liqueurs, Cordials

Brandies.

Armagnac. Superior French brandy.

Calvados. Very fine apple brandy.

Cognac. The very best brandy in the world, originating from the district of Cognac.

Framboise. Delicious, rich, colorless brandy made from distilled raspberries.

Mirabelle. Alsatian brandy made from yellow plums.

Kirsch. Dry, colorless brandy made from dark, sour cherries and characterized by a piquant, slightly bitter almond flavor.

Liqueurs and cordials. (Sweetened, flavored and sometimes artificially colored.)

Benedictine. Amber-colored liqueur made with a variety of herbs and characterized by its delicacy.

Chartreuse. Made with a cognac base and with a mixture of many aromatic herbs. There are green and yellow varieties of this unusual liqueur, the green containing more alcohol than the yellow.

Cointreau. Colorless, rich liqueur of subtle orange flavor.

Crème de menthe. Strongly peppermint-flavored liqueur which is available in luminous green or colorless varieties.

Grand Marnier. Strongly orange-flavored liqueur made with a cognac base.

Beers

Bière blonde. Light beer or ale.

Bière brune. Dark beer or stout.

Glossary of General Wine Terms

Vin blanc. White wine.

Vin borru. Light, young Burgundy often available in restaurants by the glass.

Vin doux. Sweet wine.

Vin fin. Fine wine.

Vin gris. Rosé wine of Alsace.

Vin jaune. Yellowish amber—colored wine resembling a dry sherry in flavor and bouquet.

Vin mousseux. Sparkling wine.

Vin ordinaire. Ordinary table wine.

Vin de paille. "Straw" wine, gray-pink in color. A sweet, rich dessert wine.

Vin du pays. Regional or local wine.

Vin rosé. Pink wine.

Vin rouge. Red wine.

Vin sec. Dry wine.

Dictionary

The gender of nouns is indicated by (m.) for masculine or (f.) for feminine if the definite article does not already indicate gender. Adjectives are given with the masculine form first, and the feminine form second, or simply with the feminine ending in parentheses. Certain words may be marked (adj.), (conj.) or (pron.) to avoid ambiguity among adjectives, conjunctions, and pronouns.

A

a   un, une

a little   un peu

a little bit of   un petit peu de

a lot of   beaucoup de

about   environ, à peu près

above   en haut

abroad   à l'étranger

Acadia   l'Acadie

Acadien   acadien(ne)

accelerator   l'accélérateur (m.)

accept   accepter

accessible   accessible

accessories   les accessoires (m.)

accident   l'accident (m.)

accompany   accompagner

accountant   le comptable

across from   en face de

action   l'action (f.)

activity   l'activité (f.)

actually   en fait

adapter   l'adaptateur (m.)

add to   ajouter à

address   l'adresse (f.)

admission price   le prix d'entrée

advance   avancer

advantage   l'avantage (m.)

adventure   l'aventure (f.)

advertisement l'annonce (f.)

advice le conseil

advise conseiller

Africa l'Afrique (f.)

African africain(e)

after après, ensuite

afternoon l'après-midi (m.)

again encore, de nouveau

against contre

age l'âge (m.)

agency l'agence (f.)

ago il y a

air conditioning la climatisation

air l'air (m.)

airline la compagnie aérienne

airport l'aéroport (m.)

aisle le couloir

alcohol l'alcool (m.)

alike semblable

Algeria l'Algérie (f.)

Algerian algérien(ne)

all tout

all inclusive tout inclus

allergic allergique

allow permettre de

almost presque

along le long de

aloud à haute voix

already déjà

also aussi

always toujours

ambulance l'ambulance (f.)

America l'Amérique (f.)

American américain(e)

among parmi

amusement le divertissement

amusement park le parc d'attractions

an un, une

and et

angle l'angle (m.)

angry en colère

animal l'animal (m.)

animation l'animation (f.)

ankle la cheville

anniversary l'anniversaire (m.)

annoy ennuyer, agacer, énerver

answer la réponse

ant la fourmi

antenna l'antenne (f.)

antibiotics les antibiotiques (m.)

antiseptic l'antiseptique (m.)

anyone quelqu'un(e)

anywhere n'importe où

apartment l'appartement (m.)

apologize s'excuser

apology l'excuse (f.)

apparatus l'appareil (m.)

appear apparaître

appendicitis l'appendicite (f.)

appendix l'appendice (m.)

appetite l'appétit (m.)

appetizers les amuse-gueule (m.)

apple la pomme

applesauce la compote de pommes

appointment le rendez-vous

approach s'approcher de

April avril

apron le tablier

archipelago l'archipel (m.)

architect l'architecte (m/f)

arm le bras

army l'armée (f.)

around autour

arrest arrêter

arrival l'arrivée (f.)

arrive arriver

art l'art (m.)

as comme

as much autant

as soon as aussitôt que

as soon as possible le plus tôt possible

ashtray le cendrier

ask (a question) poser

ask for demander

asparagus l'asperge (f.)

aspirin l'aspirine (f.)

assistance l'aide (f.)

astonish étonner

at à

at first d'abord

at last enfin

at least au moins

at most au plus

at sign (@) l'arobase

atheist l'athée (m/f)

ATM le distributeur automatique, le DAB

attachment la pièce jointe

attack l'attaque (f.)

DICTIONARY

attempt essayer
attract attirer
August août
aunt la tante
Australia l'Australie (f.)
Australian australien(ne)
authority l'autorité (f.)
automatic automatique
autumn l'automne (m.)
average la moyenne
avoid éviter
awkward délicat(e), maladroit(e)

B

baby le bébé
baby teeth les dents de lait
Bachelor's degree la licence, le baccalauréat (Quebec)
back le dos
backgammon le backgammon, le trictac
backwards en arrière
bacon le bacon
bad mauvais(e)
badly mal
bag le sac, le cornet (Eastern France& Switzerland)

baggage le baggage
baggage room la consigne
baker le boulanger, la boulangère
bakery la boulangerie
balcony le balcon
bald chauve
ball le ballon, la balle
banana la banane
band-aid le pansement
bandage le bandage
bank (river) la rive
bank (building) la banque
bar le bar
barn la grange
barracks la caserne
bartender le barman
baseball le baseball
basketball le basket
bath le bain
bath mat le tapis de bain
bath towel la serviette de bain, l'essuie (m.) de bain (Belgium)
bathe baigner
bathroom (public) les toilettes, les WC
bathroom la salle de bains

bathtub la baignoire

battery la pile, la batterie

battle la bataille

bay la baie

be être

beach la plage

beach chair le transat

beach umbrella le parasol

bean le haricot

bear l'ours (m.)

beard la barbe

beautiful beau, belle

beauty la beauté

beauty mark le grain de beauté

become devenir

bed le lit

bedroom la chambre

beef le bœuf

beer la bière

beer mug la chope à bière

before avant

begin to commencer à, se mettre à

beginning le commencement

behind derrière

Belgian belge

Belgium la Belgique

believe croire

bell la clochette

bell pepper le poivron

belly le ventre

belong to appartenir à

below en bas, au-dessous

belt la ceinture

bench le banc

besides d'ailleurs

best le/la mieux

better meilleur

between entre

beverage la boisson

bike le vélo

biking le cyclisme

bill (banknote) le billet

bill (restaurant) l'addition (f.)

bill (for services rendered) la facture, la note

billion le milliard

biology la biologie

bird l'oiseau (m.)

birth la naissance

birthday l'anniversaire (m.)

bite la morsure

black noir(e)

blanket   la couverture
bleed   saigner
blister   l'ampoule (f.)
blog   le blog, le blogue
blond   blond(e)
blood   le sang
blood group   le groupe sanguin
blood test   la prise de sang
blouse   le chemisier
blow   souffler
blow one's nose   se moucher
blow-dry   le brushing
blue   bleu(e)
blueberry   la myrtille, le bleuet (Quebec)
blurry   flou(e)
board   la planche
board game   le jeu de société
boarding card   la carte d'embarquement
boat   le bateau
boat (Paris sight-seeing)   le bateau-mouche
bobby pin   l'épingle (f.) à cheveux
body   le corps
bone   l'os (m.)

book (reservation)   réserver
book   le livre
booklet (of tickets)   le carnet de tickets
bookmark   le marque-page
bookstore   la librairie
boot   la botte
bore   ennuyer
borrow   emprunter
botanical garden   le jardin botanique
bottle   la bouteille
bottom   le fond
bouncer (bar)   le videur
bowling   le bowling
box (in theater)   la loge
box   la boîte
boxers (underwear)   le caleçon
boy   le garçon
boyfriend   le copain, le chum (Quebec)
bra   le soutien-gorge
bracelet   le bracelet
braces   l'appareil dentaire (m.)
brakes   les freins (m.)
bread   le pain
break   casser, briser

breakfast le petit déjeuner, le déjeuner (Quebec, Belgium, Switzerland)

breathe respirer

bridge le pont

briefs (underwear) le slip

bring apporter

British britannique

broadcast diffuser

broken cassé(e)

broken down en panne

broom le balai

brother le frère

brother-in-law le beau-frère

brown brun(e), marron

bruise le bleu, l'ecchymose (f.)

brush la brosse

Buddhist bouddhiste

build bâtir

building le bâtiment

burn brûler

bury enterrer

bus (local) l'autobus (m.)

bus (long-distance) l'autocar (m.)

bus station la gare routière

bus stop l'arrêt de bus (m.)

bush le buisson

business les affaires (f.)

busy occupé(e)

but mais

butcher le boucher

butcher shop la boucherie

butter le beurre

buy acheter

by par

by airmail par avion

'bye salut

C

cabbage le chou

café le café

cake le gâteau

calendar le calendrier

call appeler

call waiting le double appel

caller ID la présentation du numéro

calm calme

camera l'appareil photo (m.)

camper le camping-car

campfire le feu de camp

camping le camping
can (be able to) pouvoir
can (of food) la boîte
can (soda) la cannette
can opener l'ouvre-boîte (m.)
Canada le Canada
Canadian canadien/ne
cancel annuler
canceled annulé(e)
candle la bougie
candy les bonbons (m.)
candy store la confiserie
canoe le canoë
cap le casquette
cape le cap
captain le capitaine
car l'automobile (f.), la voiture
car (train) le wagon
cardigan le gilet
care le soin
carrot la carotte
carry porter
carry-on bag le bagage à main
case le cas
cash les espèces (f.)
cash register la caisse
castle le château

cat le chat
catch attraper
cathedral la cathédrale
Catholic catholique
cauliflower le chou-fleur
cave la caverne
cavity la carie
celebrate fêter, célébrer
cell phone le téléphone portable, le cellulaire (Quebec), le natel (Switzerland)
cemetery le cimetière
cent la centime
centimeter le centimètre
century le siècle
cereal les céréales (f.)
certainly certainement
chain la chaîne
chair la chaise
chalk la craie
champagne le champagne
change changer
change (coins) la monnaie
charge (extra) le supplément
cheap bon marché
check (baggage) enregistrer

check (bank) le chèque
check (restaurant) l'addition (m.)
check verifier
check-in l'enregistrement (m.)
check-in time l'heure (f.) limite d'arrivée
check-out time l'heure (f.) limite de départ
checked baggage le bagage de soute
checkers les dames
cheek la joue
cheese le fromage
chemistry la chimie
cherry la cerise
chess les échecs (m.)
chest la poitrine
chestnut la châtaigne, le marron
chew mâcher
chewing gum le chewing-gum
chicken le poulet
child l'enfant (m/f)
child seat le siège-bébé
chili pepper le piment
chill le coup de froid
chin le menton
chocolate le chocolat

chocolate croissant le pain au chocolat
chocolate mousse la mousse au chocolat
choice le choix
choose choisir
Christian chrétien(ne)
church l'église (f.)
cigar le cigare
cigarette la cigarette
cinema le cinéma
circle le cercle
city la ville
city center le centre-ville
civil servant le/la fonctionnaire
civil union l'union civile (f.), le PACS (France, Switzerland)
clean nettoyer
cleaning (teeth) le détartrage
cleaning kit le kit de nettoyage
cleanser le nettoyant
clear (vision) net(te)
clever malin (m.), maligne (f.)
climate le climat
climbing l'escalade (f.).
clock l'horloge (m.)

DICTIONARY

close fermer
closed fermé(e)
clothes les vêtements (m.)
clothes dryer la sèche-linge, la sécheuse (Quebec)
clothing store le magasin de vêtements
cloud le nuage
cloudy nuageux
coal le charbon
coast la côte
coaster le sous-verre
coat le manteau
coat room le vestiaire
cockroach le cafard
cocktail le cocktail
cod la morue
coffee with a dash of milk le café noisette
coffee with cream le café crème
coffee with hot water le café allongé / américain
coffee with milk le café au lait
cognac le cognac
coin la pièce
cold froid(e)
cold le froid
cold (illness) le rhume

collar le col
collar bone la clavicule
colleague le/la collègue
collect call l'appel (m.) en PCV
color la couleur
comb le peigne
come venir
come back revenir
come in entrer
comedy la comédie
committee le comité
company la compagnie
compare to comparer à
compass la boussole
competition la concurrence, le concours
complain about se plaindre de
computer l'ordinateur (m.)
computer science l'informatique (m.)
concert le concert
conclusion la fin
condom le préservatif
confess avouer
confidence la confiance
confuse confondre
congratulate féliciter

constantly constamment

constipation la constipation

consulate le consulat

contact le contact

contact lens (soft, hard) les lentilles (f.) (souples, dures)

contact lens solution la solution d'entretien pour les lentilles

contacts case l'étui (m.) de lentilles

contents le contenu

continue continuer

contract le contrat

cook cuisiner, faire cuire

cool frais, fraîche

copy copier

copy l'exemplaire (m.)

cord la corde

cork le bouchon

corkscrew le tire-bouchon

corn le maïs

corner le coin

correct corriger

correction fluid le correcteur liquide

cost coûter

cotton le coton

cough la toux

cough tousser

count compter

country le pays

countryside la campagne

courage le courage

courtyard la cour

cousin le cousin, la cousine

cover charge le couvert

cover with couvrir de

cow la vache

crab le crabe

cramp la crampe

crazy fou, folle

cream la crème

credit le crédit

credit card la carte de crédit

crew l'équipage (m.)

crime le crime

crisis la crise

criticism la critique

criticize critiquer

croissant le croissant

cross la croix

cross traverser

crosswalk le passage pour piétons

crowd la foule

cruise la croisière

crush écraser
cry pleurer
cucumber le concombre
cuisine la cuisine
cure guérir
curling iron le fer à friser
curly bouclé(e)
currency la monnaie
cushion le coussin
custom la coutume
customs la douane
cut couper
cute mignon(ne)
cylinder le cylindre

D

dad le papa
damage le dommage
dance la danse
dance hall le dancing
danger le danger
dark foncé(e)
darkness l'obscurité (f.)
dartboard la cible
darts les fléchettes (f.)
daughter la fille
daughter-in-law la belle-fille
day le jour, la journée

day after tomorrow après-demain
day before yesterday avant-hier
dead mort(e)
dead (battery) à plat
death la mort
debt la dette
decade la décennie
decaf coffee le café déca
December décembre
decide to décider de
deck (boat) le pont
deck of cards le jeu de cartes
declare déclarer
decorate décorer
degree le degré
delayed en retard
demand exiger
dental floss le fil dentaire
dentist le/la dentiste
dentures le dentier
deodorant le déodorant
department store le grand magasin
departure le départ
depend upon dépendre de

depth la profondeur

describe décrire

desert abandonner

desert le désert

dessert le dessert

detail le détail

detective film le polar

detergent la lessive

determine déterminer

develop se développer

development le développement

dew la rosée

diabetic diabétique

diaper la couche

diarrhea la diarrhée

dice les dés

dictionary le dictionnaire

die from mourir de

diesel le diesel, le gasoil

different différent(e)

difficulty la difficulté

digest digérer

digital camera l'appareil photo numérique

diminish diminuer

dine dîner

dine in manger sur place

dining car le wagon-restaurant

dining room la salle à manger

dinner le dîner, le souper (Quebec, Belgium, Switzerland)

direct direct(e)

direction la direction

directly directement

disabled handicapé(e)

disappear disparaître

disaster le désastre

discovery la découverte

discuss discuter

disembark débarquer

disguise oneself se déguiser

disgust le dégoût

dish towel le torchon, l'essuie (f.) de cuisine (Belgium)

dishes la vaisselle

dishwasher le lave-vaisselle

dishwasher soap le détergent pour lave-vaisselle

dishwashing soap le liquide vaisselle

disinfect désinfecter

disposable camera

l'appareil (m.) photo jetable

disposable contacts les lentilles (f.) jetables

dissolve dissoudre

distance la distance

distant éloigné(e)

distinguish distinguer

distribute distribuer

disturb déranger

ditch le fossé

dive plonger

divorced divorcé(e)

do faire

do without se passer de

dock le quai

doctor le/la médecin

doctorate le doctorat

document le document

documentary le documentaire

dog le chien

doll la poupée

dollar le dollar

dominoes les dominos (m.)

dotted à pois

double espresso le grand café

doubt le doute

download télécharger

downstairs en bas

downtown le centre-ville

dozen la douzaine

draft beer la pression

drama le drame

draw (sketch) dessiner

dream le rêve

dress la robe

drill la perceuse

drink boire

drink la boisson

drinking water l'eau (f.) potable

drive conduire

driver (computer) le pilote

driver (vehicle) le conducteur

driver's license le permis de conduire

drop laisser tomber

drop la goutte

drown se noyer

drugs (illicit) la drogue

drunk ivre

dry sécher

dry cleaner's le pressing, le nettoyeur (Quebec)

DSL l'ADSL (m.)

dubbed doublé(e)

duck le canard

dust la poussière

dustpan la pelle à poussière

DVD player le lecteur de DVD

dye teindre

dysentery la dysenterie

E

e-mail le mail, le mél, le courriel (Quebec)

ear l'oreille (f.)

earache l'otite (f.)

early tôt

earn gagner

earplugs les bouchons (m.) d'oreille

earrings les boucles (f.) d'oreille

earth la terre

east l'est (m.)

easy facile

eat manger

economy class la classe économique

edge le bord

effort l'effort (m.)

egg l'œuf (m.)

eggs (scrambled, fried) les œufs (brouillés, au plat)

eggs (soft-boiled, hard-boiled) les œufs (à la coque, durs)

eight huit

eighteen dix-huit

eighteenth dix-huitième

eighth huitième

eighty quatre-vingts (France, Belgium, & Quebec), huitante (Switzerland: Fribourg, Valais, Vaud)

eighty-one quatre-vingt-un (France, Belgium, & Quebec), huitante et un (Switzerland: Fribourg, Valais, Vaud)

eighty-two quatre-vingt-deux (France, Belgium, & Quebec), huitante-deux (Switzerland: Fribourg, Valais, Vaud)

elbow le coude

electric burners les plaques (f.) électriques

electricity l'électricité (f.)

electronics store le magasin d'électronique

elephant l'éléphant (m.)

DICTIONARY

elevator l'ascenseur (m.)
eleven onze
eleventh onzième
elsewhere ailleurs
embassy l'ambassade (f.)
embrace embrasser
emergency le cas urgent
emergency exit la sortie de secours
emergency room la salle d'urgences
employment l'emploi (m.)
empty vide
encounter la rencontre
end la fin, le bout
endive l'endive (f.)
enemy l'ennemi(e) (m/f)
engine le moteur
engineer l'ingénieur (m.), l'ingénieure (f.)
engineering l'ingénierie (f.)
England l'Angleterre (f.)
English anglais(e)
enjoy your meal bon appétit
enough assez
enter entrer dans
enterprise l'entreprise (f.)

entertainment le divertissement
entrance l'entrée (f.)
envelope l'enveloppe (f.)
environment l'environnement (m.), le milieu
envy l'envie (f.)
equality l'égalité (f.)
equipment l'outillage (m.)
equipped équipé(e
erase effacer
eraser la gomme, l'efface (m.) (Quebec)
error l'erreur (f.)
especially surtout
espresso le café
euro l'euro (m.)
Europe l'Europe (f.)
European européen(ne)
even même
evening le soir; la soirée
event l'événement (f.)
everything tout
everywhere partout
evidently évidemment
exactly justement
exaggerate exagérer
examination l'examen (m.)

example l'exemple (m.)
except sauf
excess l'excédent (m.)
exchange l'échange (m.)
exchange office le bureau de change
exchange rate le taux d'échange
excuse l'excuse (f.)
exhibition l'exposition (f.)
exist exister
existence l'existence (f.)
exit la sortie
expect attendre
expense la dépense
expensive cher(e)
explain expliquer
explanation l'explication (f.)
external hard drive le disque dur externe
extinguish éteindre
extremely extrêmement
eye l'œil (m.)
eyebrow le sourcil
eyedrops les gouttes (f.) pour les yeux, le collyre
eyelash le cil
eyelid la paupière
eyes les yeux

F

fabric le tissu, l'étoffe (f.)
fabric softener l'assouplissant (m.)
face le visage
fact le fait
factory l'usine (f.)
faint s'évanouir
fake faux, fausse
fall tomber
fall asleep s'endormir
fall ill tomber malade
fall in love with tomber amoureux de
family la famille
far from loin de
far-sighted hypermétrope
farm la ferme
fast-food restaurant le fast-food
fat gros(se)
father le père
father-in-law le beau-père
faucet le robinet
fault la faute
fax le fax
fear la peur, la crainte
feather la plume

DICTIONARY

February février
fee le frais
feed nourrir
feel se sentir
ferry le ferry, le traversier (Quebec)
fever la fièvre
few quelques
field le champ
fifteen quinze
fifteenth quinzième
fifth cinquième
fifty cinquante
file (document) le dossier
file (tool) la lime
filing cabinet le classeur
fill (gas tank) faire le plein
fill with remplir de
filling (tooth) le plombage
film (camera) la pellicule
film (movie) le film
finally enfin
find trouver
fine (satisfactory) bien
finger le doigt
finger wave la mise en pli
finish finir

fire le feu
fire hydrant la bouche à incendie
firetruck le camion de pompiers
first (of all) d'abord
first premier, première
first class la première classe
first-aid kit la trousse de premiers secours
fish le poisson
fish merchant le poissonier
fish pêcher
fist le poing
five cinq
fixed rate plan le forfait
flag le drapeau
flash drive la clé USB
flashlight la torche
flat plat(e)
flat tire le pneu crevé
flats (ballet shoes) les ballerines (f.)
flea market le marché aux puces
flight le vol
flip-flops les tongs (m.)
floor le plancher
floor (story) l'étage (m.)

flow couler
flower la fleur
flower shop le fleuriste
flowery à fleurs
flu la grippe
fly la mouche
fly voler
flyswatter la tapette à mouches
fog le brouillard
fold le pli
follow suivre
food la nourriture
food poisoning l'intoxication (f.) alimentaire
foot le pied
football le football américain
for pour
forbid défendre
forbidden interdit(e)
force la force
forecast (weather) les prévisions (f.), la météo
forehead le front
forest la forêt
forget oublier
forgive pardonner
fork la fourchette

fortunately heureusement
forty quarante
forward en avant
found (establish) fonder
fountain la fontaine
four quatre
fourteen quatorze
fourteenth quatorzième
fourth quatrième
fox le renard
fracture la fracture
frame la monture
franc le franc
France la France
freckle la tache de rousseur
free gratuit; libre
freeze geler
French français(e)
French fries les frites (f.)
fresh water l'eau (f.) douce
Friday vendredi
fried frit(e)
friend l'ami (m.), l'amie (f.)
friendship l'amitié (f.)
frighten effrayer
frilly à froufrous
from de

251

DICTIONARY

from now on désormais

from time to time de temps en temps

front le front

frozen (computer) bloqué(e)

fruit le fruit

fruit juice le jus de fruit

fruit salad la salade de fruits

fruitcake le cake aux fruits

fuel le combustible, le carburant

full plein(e)

fun amusant(e)

funny drôle

fur la fourrure

furnished meublé(e)

future l'avenir (m.)

G

game le jeu

game show le jeu télévisé

garage le garage

garbage les ordures (f.), les vidanges (f.) (Quebec)

garbage can la poubelle

garden le jardin

garlic l'ail (m.)

gas station la station service

gasoline l'essence (f.)

gate le portail, la barrière

gate (airport) la porte d'embarquement

gauze la gaze

gear lever le levier de vitesse

geography la géographie

gesture le geste

get married se marier

get off descendre

get on embarquer

get rid of se débarrasser de

gift le cadeau

giraffe la girafe

girl la fille

girlfriend la copine, la blonde (Quebec)

give donner

glad content(e)

glass le verre

glasses les lunettes (f.)

glasses case l'étui (m.) de lunettes

glove le gant

go aller

go away s'en aller

go out sortir

go to bed se coucher

goat la chèvre

goddaughter la filleule

godfather le parrain

godmother la marraine

godson le filleul

gold l'or (m.)

golden doré(e)

golf le golf

golf club la crosse de golf

good bon, bonne

good evening bonsoir

good morning bonjour

good night bonne nuit

good-bye au revoir

goose l'oie (f.)

govern gouverner

government le gouvernement

GPS le système GPS

grandchildren les petits-enfants

granddaughter la petite-fille

grandfather le grand-père, le pépé

grandmother la grand-mère, la mamie

grandparents les grands-parents

grandson le petit-fils

grape le raisin

grapefruit le pamplemousse

grass l'herbe (f.)

gray gris(e)

Great Britain la Grande-Bretagne

green vert(e)

greet saluer

greeting card la carte de vœux

grinding (sound) le grincement

grocery store l'épicerie (f.), le dépanneur (Quebec)

ground beef le steak haché

group le groupe

growth la croissance

guess deviner

guide le guide

guided tour la visite guidée

gulf la golfe

253

gums les gencives (f.)

gun le fusil

H

hail la grêle

hair les cheveux

hair salon le salon de coiffure

hair stylist le coiffeur, la coiffeuse

haircut la coupe de cheveux

hairdryer le sèche-cheveux, le fœhn (Switzerland)

half la moitié

half pension la demi-pension

half-brother le demi-frère

half-sister la demi-sœur

ham le jambon

hammer le marteau

hand la main

handbag le sac à main

handful la poignée

handicapped handicapé(é)

handkerchief le mouchoir

handle (door) la poignée de porte, la clenche (Belgium)

handlebar le guidon

handsome beau

hang (suspend) accrocher, suspendre

hangers les cintres (m.)

happen arriver

happiness le bonheur

happy heureux, heureuse

hard dur(e)

hardly à peine

hardware le matériel

hat (standard) le chapeau

hat (wool/knit) le bonnet, la tuque (Quebec)

hate la haine

have avoir

hazelnut la noisette

he il

head la tête

headache le mal de tête

headlight le phare

headset le casque

health insurance l'assurance (f.) maladie

health la santé

hear entendre

hearing l'ouïe (f.)

hearing aid l'appareil (m.) acoustique

heart le cœur

heat la chaleur

heel le talon

height la hauteur

helicopter l'hélicoptère (m.)

hello bonjour, allô

helmet le casque

help aider

help (in danger) au secours

hem raccourcir

her (adj.) son, sa, ses

her (pron.) la, lui

herb l'herbe (f.)

herbal tea l'infusion (f.), la tisane

here ici, là

hers le sien, la sienne, les siens, les siennes

hesitate hésiter

hi salut

hide cacher

high haut(e)

high blood pressure l'hypertension (f.) artérielle

high heels les talons (m.) hauts, les escarpins (m.)

high tide la marée haute

high-speed Internet Internet à haut débit

high-speed train le train à grande vitesse

highlighter le surligneur

highlights (hair) les balayages (m.)

highway l'autoroute (f.)

hiking la randonnée

hill la colline

him le, lui

hip la hanche

hire (rent) louer

his (adj.) son, sa, ses

his (pron.) le sien, la sienne, les siens, les siennes

history l'histoire (f.)

hives l'urticaire (f.)

hockey le hockey

hockey puck le palet, la rondelle (Quebec)

hoe la binette, la houe

hold tenir

hole le trou

homosexual homosexuel(le)

honor l'honneur (m.)

hook le crochet

hope l'espoir (m.), l'espérance (f.)

horror movie le film d'horreur

horse le cheval
hose le tuyau
hospital l'hôpital (m.)
hot chaud(e)
hot chocolate le chocolat chaud
hot water l'eau (f.) chaude
hot water bottle la bouillote
hotel l'hôtel (m.)
hour l'heure (f.)
house la maison
household cleaning products les produits (m.) ménagers
housework le ménage
how comment
how far à quelle distance
how long combien de temps
how much combien
humid humide
hundredth centième
hunger la faim
hurry se dépêcher
hurt faire mal; blesser
husband le mari
hypothermia l'hypothermie (f.)

I

I je
ice la glace
ice cream la glace
ice cube le glaçon
ice skate le patin à glace
iced tea le thé glacé
idea l'idée (f.)
identification card la carte d'identité
ill malade
illness la maladie
imagine imaginer
imam l'imam (m.)
imitate imiter
immediately tout de suite
improve améliorer
in en, dans
in front of devant
in general en général
in the middle of au milieu de
included compris(e)
increase augmenter
indeed vraiment, en vérité
independent film le film indépendant
indicate indiquer

indigestion l'indigestion (f.)

infected infecté(e)

infection l'infection (f.)

information les renseignements

inhabit habiter

inhabitant l'habitant (m.)

inherit hériter

injured blessé(e)

ink l'encre (f.)

ink cartridge la cartouche d'encre

inn l'auberge (f.)

insect l'insecte (m.)

insect bite la piqûre

insect bite lotion la lotion contre les piqûres d'insecte

insect repellent le produit anti-insecte

inside dedans, à l'intérieur

instrument l'instrument (m.)

insult insulter

insurance l'assurance (f.)

insure assurer

insured valeur declaré(e)

intelligent intelligent(e)

interest l'intérêt (m.)

intermission l'entr'acte (m.)

international international(e)

international call l'appel (m.) international

Internet Internet (m.)

Internet café le cybercafé

Internet user l'internaute (m/f)

interpreter l'interprète (m/f)

interrupt interrompre

intestinal problems les problèmes (m.) intestinaux

intestines les intestins (m.)

introduce présenter

invite inviter

iodine l'iode (m.)

Ireland l'Irlande (f.)

Irishman irlandais(e)

iron le fer à repasser

ironing board la planche à repasser

island l'île (f.)

it le, la

it is c'est

it is not ce n'est pas

its son, sa, ses

J

jack le cric
jacket la veste
jam la confiture
January janvier
jar le bocal, le pot
jaw la mâchoire
jealous jalous(e)
jeans le jean
jersey le maillot, le chandail de joueur (Quebec)
jet lag le décalage horaire
jet ski le jet-ski
jewelry les bijoux (m.)
jewelry store la bijouterie
Jewish juif, juive
job le travail
join joindre
joint l'articulation (f.)
joke la plaisanterie
journalist le/la journaliste
journey le voyage
joy la joie
judge juger
judgment le jugement
July juillet

jump sauter
jumper cables les câbles (m.) de démarrage
June juin
jungle la jungle

K

keep maintenir; garder
kettle la bouilloire
key la clé
key ring le porte-clés
keyboard le clavier
kick donner un coups de pied
kidney le rein
kill tuer
kilogram le kilogramme
kilometer le kilomètre
kind l'espèce (f.), le genre
kiss embrasser
kitchen la cuisine
kitchen towel le torchon
knee le genou
knick-knack le bibelot
knife le couteau
knit tricoter
knitting needle l'aiguille (f.) à tricoter
knock frapper

knock down renverser

knot le nœud

know savoir; connaître

knowledge la connaissance

knuckle l'articulation (f.) du doigt

L

label l'étiquette (f.)

lactose intolerant l'intolérance (f.) au lactose

ladder l'échelle

lake le lac

lamb l'agneau (m.)

lane la voie

language la langue; le langage

laptop computer l'ordinateur (m.) portable

large grand(e)

last (in a series) dernier, dernière

last (in the past) passé(e)

last durer

last night hier soir

late en retard

later plus tard

laugh rire

laundromat la laverie, la launderette (Quebec)

laundry room la buanderie

laundry service la blanchisserie

law la loi

lawyer l'avocat(e)

laxative le laxatif

layover la correspondance

lazy paresseux, paresseuse

lead le plomb

leak la fuite

learn to apprendre à

leather le cuir

leave (depart) partir

leave (something) laisser

lecture la conférence

leek le poireau

left la gauche

leg la jambe

lemon le citron

lemon soda le limonade

lemonade le citron pressé

lend prêter

length la longueur

lens l'objectif (m.)

lesbian lesbienne

less moins
lesson la leçon
let laisser
letter la lettre
letter opener le coupe-papier
lettuce la laitue
level le niveau
library la bibliothèque, la mediathèque
lie le mensonge
life la vie
lifeboat le canot de sauvetage
life preserver la ceinture de sauvetage
light la lumière
light (weight) léger, légère
light (color) clair(e)
lightbulb l'ampoule (f.)
light custard cream la crème anglaise
lighter le briquet
lighthouse le phare
lightning l'éclair (m.)
like aimer
lime le citron vert
limp boîter
line la ligne

linen le linge
link le lien
lip la lèvre
lipstick le rouge à lèvres
list la liste
listen écouter
liter le litre
literature la littérature
little peu
live habiter; vivre
liver le foie
living room le salon
lobster le homard; la langouste
local anesthesia l'anesthésie (f.) locale
local call l'appel (m.) local
lock la serrure
locked fermé(e) à clé
locked (cell phone) bloqué(é)
locker room la consigne
long long(ue)
look at regarder
look after s'occuper de
look for chercher
lose perdre
loss la perte
lost perdu(e)

lost and found le bureau des objets trouvés
lottery la loterie, le loto
lottery tickets les tickets (m.) de loto
loud bruyant(e)
love aimer
love l'amour (m.)
low bas, basse
low tide la marée basse
lower baisser
lunch le déjeuner, le dîner (Quebec, Belgium, Switzerland)
lung le poumon
Luxembourg le Luxembourg
(of, from) Luxembourg luxembourgeois(e)
luxury le luxe

M

machine la machine
magazine le magazine
magnet l'aimant (m.), le magnet
mailbox la boîte à lettres
majority la majorité
make faire
make a mistake se tromper

make sure of s'assurer de
make-up le maquillage
man l'homme (m.)
manage (direct) diriger
manager le directeur, le gérant
manicure la manucure
manner la manière, le façon
manual manuel(le)
manufacture fabriquer
many beaucoup
map la carte, le plan
March mars
market le marché
married marié(e)
marry épouser
mass la messe
Master's degree le master, la maîtrise (Quebec)
matches les allumettes (f.)
material (things) le matériel
math les mathématiques (f.)
matinee la matinée
matter la matière
May mai
maybe peut-être

DICTIONARY

me   me, moi

meal   le repas

mean   méchant(e)

mean   vouloir dire

means   le moyen

meanwhile   en attendant

measure   mesurer

measurement   la dimension

meat   la viande

mechanic   le mécanicien

medicine   le médicament

medium (meat)   à point

medium (size)   moyen(ne)

medium rare (meat)   saignant

meet   rencontrer

meeting   la réunion

melon   le melon

melt   fondre

member   le membre

memory   la mémoire

memory card   la carte mémoire

menstrual cramps   les règles (f.) douleureuses

mention   mentionner

menu   la carte

message   le message

metal   le métal

meter   le mètre

microwave   le four à micro-ondes

middle   le centre, le milieu

midnight   minuit

migraine   la migraine

mild   doux, douce

millenium   le millénaire

million   le million

mine (pron.)   le mien, la mienne, les miens, les miennes

minimum   le minimum

minivan   le monospace

minute   la minute

miss   manquer

mistake   l'erreur (f.)

mitten   la moufle

mom   la maman

moment   le moment

monastery   le monastère

Monday   lundi

money   l'argent (m.)

money order   le mandat

monitor   l'écran (m.)

month   le mois

monument   le monument

moon   la lune

more   plus

morning   le matin

Morocco le Maroc
Moroccan marocain(e)
mosque la mosquée
mother la mère
mother-in-law la belle-mère
mountain la montagne
mountain climbing l'alpinisme (m.)
mouse la souris
mousepad le tapis de souris
mouth la bouche
mouthwash le bain de bouche
move (budge) bouger, remuer
move (to new place) déménager
movement le mouvement
movie theater le cinéma
MP3 player le lecteur mp3
much beaucoup
mud la boue, la vase
mug la grande tasse, le mug
muscle le muscle
museum le musée
mushroom le champignon

music la musique
Muslim musulman(e)
mussel la moule
must devoir
mustache la moustache
my mon, ma, mes

N

nail (body) l'ongle (m.)
nail (metal) le clou
nail clippers les coupe-ongles (m.)
nail file la lime à ongles
nail polish remover le dissolvant
name le nom
napkin la serviette, la napkine (Quebec)
nation la nation
national national(e)
nationality la nationalité
nature la nature
nausea la nausée
near près de
near-sighted myope
neck le cou
necklace le collier
need avoir besoin de
needle l'aiguille (f.)
nephew le neveu

nerve le nerf

never jamais

new nouveau, nouvelle

New Zealand la Nouvelle-Zélande

(of, from) New Zealand néo-zélandais(e)

news les nouvelles (f.), les info (f.)

newspaper le journal

newstand le kiosque

next prochain(e)

next to à côté de

nice gentil(le)

niece la nièce

night la nuit

nightclub la boîte de nuit

nightgown la chemise de nuit

nine neuf

nineteen dix-neuf

nineteenth dix-neuvième

ninety quatre-vingt-dix (France & Quebec) nonante (Acadia, Belgium & Switzerland)

ninety-one quatre-vingt-onze (France & Quebec), nonante et un (Acadia, Belgium & Switzerland)

ninety-two quatre-vingt-douze (France & Quebec), nonante-deux (Acadia, Belgium & Switzerland)

ninth neuvième

no non

noise le bruit

non-smoking non-fumeur

noodles les nouilles (f.)

noon midi

north le nord

northeast le nord-est

northwest le nord-ouest

nose le nez

not ne... pas

not at all pas du tout

not bad pas mal

not even même pas

not yet pas encore

notepad le bloc-notes

nothing rien

notice (warning) l'avis (m.)

November novembre

now maintenant

nowhere nulle part

number le nombre, le chiffre, le numéro

nurse l'infirmier (m.), l'infirmière (f.)

nut (metal) l'écrou (m.)
nut (walnut) la noix

O

ocean l'océan (m.)
October octobre
of de
of course bien sûr
offer offrir
often souvent
oil l'huile (f.)
ointment la pommade
old vieux, vieille
old city la vieille ville
olive l'olive (f.)
omelet l'omelette (f.)
on sur
on time à l'heure
one un(e)
one hundred cent
one thousand mille
one-way l'aller simple (m.)
onion l'oignon (m
only seulement
open ouvert(e)
open air market le marché en plein air
opening l'ouverture (f.)
opera l'opéra
optician l'opticien(ne)

orange orange
orchestra l'orchestre (m.)
order (command) l'ordre (m.)
order (goods, meal) la commande
origin l'origine (f.)
original original(e)
our notre, nos
ours le nôtre, la nôtre, les nôtres
out of gas en panne d'essence
out of order hors service
outfit (clothing) l'ensemble (m.)
outside dehors, à l'extérieur
oven le four
over au-dessus
over there là-bas
owe devoir
own posséder
owner le propriétaire
ox le bœuf
oyster l'huître (f.)

P

pacifier la tétine
pack le paquet

package le colis
paddle la pagaie
paddle boat le pédalo
padlock le cadenas
pail le seau, la chaudière (Quebec)
pain la douleur
painting la peinture
pair la paire
pajamas le pyjama
palace le palais
panties les culottes (f.)
pants le pantalon (m.)
paper le papier
paper towel l'essuie-tout (m.)
paperclip le trombone
pardon pardonner
parents les parents (m.)
park le parc
parking lot le parking
parsley le persil
part (hair) la raie
part (of whole) la partie
partner (spouse) le conjoint, la conjointe
party (politics) le parti
pass passer
passport le passeport

password le mot de passe
past le passé
pasta les pâtes (f.)
pastor le pasteur
pastry la viennoiserie, la couque (Belgium)
pastry shop la pâtisserie
path le sentier
pattern le motif
pavement la chaussée
pay payer
peace la paix
peach la pêche
peanuts les cacahuètes (f.) (Europe), les arachides (Quebec)
peas les petits pois (m.)
pedal la pédale
pedestrian crossing le passage piéton
pedicure la pédicurie
pen le stylo
pencil le crayon
pencil bag la trousse
pencil sharpener le taille-crayon
penicillin la pénicilline
peninsula la péninsule
people les gens, le peuple

pepper le poivre

per par

perfume le parfum

perhaps peut-être

person la personne

personal personnel(le)

pharmacy la pharmacie

Ph.D. le doctorat

phone card la télécarte

phone book l'annuaire (m.)

photocopy la photocopie

photograph la photographie

phrase l'expression (f.)

phrase book le manuel de conversation

picture frame le cadre photo

pie la tarte

piece le morceau

piercing le piercing

pig le cochon

pigeon le pigeon

pill la pilule

pillow case la taie d'oreiller

pillow l'oreiller (m.)

pin l'épingle (f.)

PIN code le code secret

pine tree le sapin

pink rose

pitcher of water la carafe d'eau

pitcher of wine le pichet de vin

pizza la pizza

place l'endroit (m.)

plaid à carreaux

plain la plaine

plane l'avion (m.)

planet la planète

plant la plante

plate l'assiette (f.)

platform le quai

play jouer

play la pièce de théâtre

playground l'aire (m.) de jeux

please (command) veuillez

please s'il vous plaît

pleasure le plaisir

pliers les pinces (f.)

pneumonia la pneumonie

poem le poème

poetry la poésie

point montrer du doigt

poison le poison

police la police

police station le commissariat de police

polite poli(e)

political science les sciences (f.) politiques

politics la politique

polo shirt le polo

pond l'étang (m.)

poor pauvre

population la population

pork le porc

port le port

possible possible

post office la poste

post office box la boîte postale, la case postale (Switzerland)

post-doctoral fellowship le stage postdoctoral

postcard la carte postale

pot la marmite, le pot

potato la pomme de terre

pour verser

poverty la pauvreté

power le pouvoir

power cord le cordon

practice la pratique, l'entraînement (m.)

pray prier

precede précéder

prefer préférer

pregnant enceinte

prejudice le préjugé

prepaid prépayé(e)

prepare préparer

prescription l'ordonnance (f.)

present (gift) le cadeau

present (time) le présent

present présent(e)

pressure la pression

pretend faire semblant

prevent empêcher

previously auparavant

price le prix

priest le prêtre

print imprimer

printer l'imprimante (f.)

prison la prison

prize le prix

probably probablement

problem le problème

product le produit

professor le/la professeur

profit le profit, le bénéfice

program le programme, l'émission (f.)

progress le progrès

promise la promesse
pronounce prononcer
proof la preuve
property la propriété
protect protéger
protest protester
Protestant protestant(e)
prove prouver
psychology la psychologie
publish publier
publisher l'éditeur (m.), l'éditrice (f.)
publishing house la maison d'édition
pudding la crème desserte; le pudding
pull tirer
pull out arracher
pump la pompe
puncture la crevaison
punish punir
punishment la punition
purchase l'achat (m.)
purple violet(te)
purpose le but
purse la pochette; le porte-monnaie; le sac à main
pursue poursuivre

push pousser
put mettre, poser
puzzle le puzzle

Q

quantity la quantité
quarter (time) le quart
Quebec le Québec
(of, from) Quebeck québécois(e)
question la question
quickly vite

R

rabbi le rabbin
rabbit le lapin
race (competition) la course
radio la radio
railroad le chemin de fer
railway station la gare ferroviaire
rain la pluie
rain pleuvoir
raincoat l'imperméable (m.)
raise (lift) lever, soulever
raise (pay) l'augmentation (f.)
raisin le raisin sec

269

rare (meat) bleu

rash l'éruption (f.) cutanée

raspberry la framboise

rat le rat

rate le prix

rattle (noise) le cliquetis

razor le rasoir

razor blade la lame de rasoir

read lire

ready prêt(e)

real vrai(e)

really vraiment

reason la raison

receipt le reçu, le ticket de caisse

receive recevoir

recently récemment

reception l'acceuil (m.)

recharge recharger

recognize reconnaître

recommend recommander

recover (get better) se remettre

rectangle le rectangle

red rouge

reduction la réduction

refrigerator le réfrigérateur

refund le remboursement

refusal le refus

regarding quant à

register enregistrer, déclarer

registered (letter) recommandé

regret regretter

relative le parent

rely on compter sur

remain rester

remainder le reste

remedy le remède

remember se souvenir de, se rappeler

remind rappeler

remove retirer, enlever

rent le loyer

rent louer

rental car la voiture de location

repair réparer

repeat répéter

repeatedly plusieurs fois

replace remplacer

reply répondre

request la demande

reservation la réservation

reserve réserver

reserved réservé(e)

respect le respect

rest le repos

rest se reposer

rest area l'aire de repos (f.)

restaurant le restaurant

result le résultat

retired à la retraite

return (give back) rendre

return (go back) retourner

return address l'expéditeur (m.)

reward la récompense

rib la côte

rice le riz

right la droite

ring (bell) sonner

ring (jewelry) la bague, l'anneau (m.)

ringtone la sonnerie

risk le risque

river le fleuve

road la route

road map la carte routière

road sign le panneau de signalisation

roast beef le rosbif

roast rôti(e)

rob voler

robe le peignoir

rock le rocher

roll rouler

rollerblade le roller

roller skate le patin à roulettes

romantic romantique

room la salle, la chambre, la cabine

root la racine

root canal le canal dentaire

rope la corde

rose la rose

roundtrip l'aller-retour (m.)

rowboat la barque

rub frotter

rubber le caoutchouc

rubber band l'élastique (m.)

rubbing alcohol l'alcool (m.) dénaturé

rude impoli(e)

rugby le rugby

ruins les ruines (f.)

rule la règle

ruler la règle, la latte (Belgium)

run courir

runny nose le nez qui coule

S

sad triste

safe sûr(e)

safe le coffre-fort

safety deposit box le coffre

safety pin l'épingle (f.) de sûreté

sail la voile

sailboat le voilier

salami le saucisson

sale la vente

salmon le saumon

salt le sel

salt water l'eau (f.) salée

sample l'échantillon (m.)

sand le sable

sandals les sandales (f.)

sandwich le sandwich

sanitary napkins les serviettes (f.) hygiéniques

sardine la sardine

Saturday samedi

sauce la sauce

sauerkraut la choucroute

sausage la saucisse

save (money) économiser, épargner

save from sauver de

saw la scie

say dire

scanner le scanner

scarf l'écharpe (f.); le foulard

school l'école (f.)

science la science

science fiction la science-fiction

scissors les ciseaux (m.)

scooter le scooter

Scotland l'Écosse (f.)

Scottish écossais(e)

scratch l'égratignure (f.)

screen l'écran (m.)

screening le dépistage

screw la vis

screwdriver le tournevis

sculpture la sculpture

sea la mer

seafood les fruits (m.) de mer

search chercher

search le recherche

search engine le moteur de recherche

seasick le mal de mer

season la saison

seat le siège, la selle

second second(e), deuxième

security camera la caméra de surveillance

security guard le gardien

see voir

seem sembler, avoir l'air

seldom rarement

sell vendre

send envoyer

Senegal le Sénégal

Senegalese sénégalais(e)

senior la personne âgée

sense le sens

sentence la phrase

separated séparé(e)

September septembre

series (television) la série

serious sérieux, sérieuse

seriously gravement

serve servir

service le service

service (religious) l'office (m.)

seven sept

seventeen dix-sept

seventeenth dix-septième

seventh septième

seventy soixante-dix (France & Quebec), septante (Acadia, Belgium & Switzerland)

seventy-one soixante-onze (France & Quebec), septante et un (Acadia, Belgium & Switzerland)

seventy-two soixante-douze (France & Quebec), septante-deux (Acadia, Belgium & Switzerland)

several plusieurs

sew coudre

sewing machine la machine à coudre

sex le sexe

shadow l'ombre (f.)

shake secouer; trembler

shampoo le shampooing

share partager

shave se raser

shaving cream la crème à raser

she elle

sheets les draps (m.)

ship expédier

ship le navire

shirt la chemise

shoe la chaussure, le soulier

shoe store le magasin de chaussures

shoelace le lacet

shop faire du shopping, magasiner (Quebec)

shop la boutique

short petit(e); court(e)

shorts le short

shot glass le verre à shooter

shoulder l'épaule (f.)

shout le cri

shovel la pelle

show le spectacle

show montrer

shower la douche

shrimp la crevette

shuttle la navette

sick malade

side effects les effets (m.) secondaires

side le côté

sidewalk le trottoir

sight la vue

sightseeing le tourisme

sign le signe

sign signer

silk la soie

silver l'argent (m.); **silver (adj.)** argenté(e)

silverware les couverts (m.), les services (Switzerland)

SIM card la carte SIM

since depuis

sing chanter

single célibataire

sink l'évier (m.), le lavabo

sister la sœur

sister-in-law la belle-sœur

sit down s'asseoir

six six

sixteen seize

sixteenth seizième

sixth sixième

sixty soixante

size la taille, la pointure

skate le patin

ski le ski

ski pole le bâton de ski

ski shoe la chaussure de ski

skiing (downhill, cross-country) le ski (de piste, de fond)

skin la peau

skirt la jupe

274

skull   le crâne

sky   le ciel

sleep   dormir

sleeping bag   le sac de couchage

sleeping pills   les somnifères (m.)

sleeve   la manche

slice   la tranche

slip   la jupette

slip   glisser

slipper   la pantoufle, le chausson

slow   lent(e)

slowly   lentement

small   petit(e)

smell   l'odeur (f.)

smile   le sourire

smoke   fumer

smoker   le fumeur

snack bar   la buvette

snack   le goûter

snail   l'escargot (m.)

snake   le serpent

sneakers   les baskets (m.)

sneeze   éternuer

snore   ronfler

snow   la neige

snowboard   le snowboard

snowglobe   la boule de neige

snowshoe   la raquette

so much   tant, tellement

soap   le savon

soap opera   le feuilleton, le téléroman (Quebec)

soccer   le foot, le soccer (Quebec)

sock   la chaussette

sofa   le canapé

soft   doux, douce

soft drink   la boisson gazeuse

software   le logiciel

soil   la terre

solution   la solution

solve   résoudre

some   du, de la, des

someone   quelqu'un(e)

something   quelque chose

sometimes   quelquefois, parfois

somewhere   quelque part

son   le fils

son-in-law   le gendre, le beau-fils

song   la chanson

soon   bientôt

sore throat   le mal de gorge

sorry désolé(e)

sound le son

soup la soupe, le potage

sour aigre

south le sud

South Africa l'Afrique (f.) du Sud

South African sud-africain(e)

southeast le sud-est

souvenir le souvenir

souvenir shop le magasin de souvenirs

space l'espace (m.)

spade la bêche

spare tire le pneu de secours

sparkling water l'eau (f.) pétillante; l'eau gazeuse

speak parler

speakers les enceintes (m.)

special spécial(e)

specialist le spécialiste

speech la parole; le discours

speed la vitesse

spell épeler

spend (money) dépenser

spend (time) passer

sphere la sphère

spider l'araignée (f.)

spinach les épinards (m.)

spine la colonne vertébrale

sponge l'éponge (f.)

spoon la cuillère

sport le sport

spouse l'époux (m.), l'épouse (f.)

sprain l'entorse (f.)

spring le printemps

square (shape) le carré

square (location) la place

squeak le bruit aigu

squid le calmar

stadium le stade

stall caler

stamp le timbre

staple l'agrafe (f.)

stapler l'agrafeuse (f.)

star l'étoile (f.)

start (begin) commencer

start (vehicle) démarrer

starter le démarreur

state l'état (m.)

station la station

station wagon le break, la familiale (Quebec)

stationery store la papeterie

statue la statue

stay rester

stay-at-home dad l'homme (m.) au foyer

stay-at-home mom la femme au foyer

steak le bifteck, le steak

steal voler

steel l'acier (m.)

steering wheel le volant

step le pas

stepbrother le demi-frère

stepdaughter la belle-fille

stepfather le beau-père

stepmother la belle-mère

stepsister la demi-sœur

stepson le beau-fils

steward le steward

still encore, toujours

still water l'eau (f.) plate

sting piquer

stockings les bas (m.)

stomach l'estomac (m.)

stomach flu la gastro

stomachache le mal de ventre

stone la pierre

stop s'arrêter

stop sign le panneau stop

store le magasin

storm l'orage (f.), la tempête

straight droit(e), raide

straight (direction) tout droit

strait le détroit

strap la bretelle

strawberry la fraise

street la rue

streetcar le tramway

stretcher la civière, le brancard

strike la grève

string la ficelle

striped à rayures

stuck (in mud) embourbé(e)

student l'étudiant(e)

study étudier

stuffed animal l'animal (m.) en peluche

stuffy nose le nez bouché

stupid stupide

subscription l'abonnement (m.)

subtitles les sous-titres (m.)

suburb la banlieue
subway le métro
success le succès
suddenly soudainement
suffer souffrir
sufficient suffisant(e)
sugar le sucre
suggestion la suggestion
suit (men) le costume
suit (women) le tailleur
summary le résumé
summer l'été (m.)
sun le soleil
sunblock l'écran (m.) solaire
sunburn le coup de soleil
sunburn ointment la lotion après-soleil
Sunday dimanche
sunflower le tournesol
sunglasses les lunettes (f.) de soleil
sunstroke l'insolation (f.)
supermarket le supermarché
support soutenir
suppose supposer
suppository le suppositoire
surf le surf

surface la surface
surprise la surprise
suspect le suspect
suspenders les bretelles (f.)
swallow avaler
swear (curse) jurer
swear (take oath) prêter serment
sweat transpirer
sweater le pull, le chandail (Quebec)
sweep balayer
sweet sucré(e)
swim nager
swimming la natation
swimsuit le maillot de bain
Swiss suisse
Switzerland la Suisse
swollen enflé(e)
synagogue la synagogue
syrup le sirop
system le système

T

T-shirt le t-shirt
tablet le cachet, le comprimé
taillight le feu arrière

take prendre
take away enlever
take out (food) emporter
tall grand(e)
tampon le tampon
tan bronzé(e)
tank top le débardeur
tape le scotch
tape measure le mètre
tart la tartelette
taste le goût
tattoo le tatouage
tax l'impôt (m.)
taxi le taxi
taxi stand la station de taxis
tea le thé
teach enseigner
teacher le/la professeur
teaspoonful la cuillerée
telephone le téléphone
telephone number le numéro de téléphone
television la télévision
tell dire, raconter
temporarily temporairement
ten dix
tennis le tennis

tennis racket la raquette de tennis
tent la tente
tenth dixième
test l'épreuve (f.)
text le texte
text message le SMS, le texto
thank you merci
that (adj.) ce, cet, cette
that (conj.) que
that (pron.) ce, ça, cela, ceci
that one celui-là, celle-la
the le, la, les
theater le théâtre
theft le vol
their leur
theirs le leur, la leur, les leurs
them les, leur
then puis, ensuite
there là, y
there is, are il y a
thermometer le thermomètre
these (adj.) ces
these (pron.) ceux, celles
they ils, elles
thief le voleur

thigh   la cuisse

thin   mince

thing   la chose

think   penser

third   troisième

thirst   la soif

thirteen   treize

thirteenth   treizième

thirty   trente

thirty-one   trente-et-un

this (adj.)   ce, cet, cette

this (pron.)   ce, ça, cela, ceci

this one   celui-ci, celle-ci

those (adj.)   ces

those (pron.)   ceux, celles

thread   le fil

threaten   menacer

three   trois

thriller   le thriller

throat   la gorge

through   à travers, par

throw   jeter, lancer

thumb   le pouce

thunder   le tonnerre

Thursday   jeudi

ticket   le billet, le ticket

ticket counter   le guichet

ticket machine   le guichet automatique

tie   la cravate

time   le temps

timetable   l'horaire (m.)

tip   le pourboire

tire   le pneu

tired   fatigué(e)

tissue   le mouchoir

tissue paper   le papier de soie

to   à; vers; chez

toast   le pain grillé

toaster   le grille-pain

tobacconist's   le tabac

today   aujourd'hui

toe   l'orteil (m.)

toenail   l'ongle (m.) de l'orteil (m.)

together   ensemble

toilet   les toilettes (f.)

toilet paper   le papier toilette

token   le jeton

tolerate   tolérer

toll   le péage

toll sticker   la vignette

tomato   la tomate

tomorrow   demain

tongue   la langue

tonight   ce soir

tonsilitis   l'angine

(f.), l'amygdalite (f.)
(Quebec)

tonsils les amygdales (f.)

too aussi; trop

too much trop

tool l'outil (m.)

tool box la boîte à outils

tooth la dent

toothache le mal de
dents

toothbrush la brosse à
dents

toothpaste le dentifrice

top le dessus

tornado la tornade

touch toucher

tough dur(e)

tourniquet le tourniquet

tow remorquer

towards vers

towel la serviette

towelettes les lingettes
(f.)

tower la tour

town la ville, la commune

town hall la mairie

toy le jouet

tractor le tracteur

trade le commerce

traffic la circulation

traffic lights le feu
tricolore

traffic sign le panneau

trailer la remorque

train le train

train station la gare
ferroviaire

translation la traduction

translator le traducteur,
la traductrice

transportation le
transport

travel voyager

traveler's checks le
chèque voyage

treatment le traitement

treaty le traité

tree l'arbre (m.)

trenchcoat le trench

trial le procès

triangle le triangle

trout la truite

truck le camion

trunk le coffre, la valise
(Quebec)

truth la vérité

try essayer

Tuesday mardi

tuna le thon

Tunisia la Tunisie

Tunisian tunisien(ne)

turkey la dinde, le dindon

turn tourner

twelfth douzième

twelve douze

twentieth vingtième

twenty vingt

twenty-one vingt-et-un

twice deux fois

twins les jumeaux (m.), les jumelles (f.)

two deux

two hundred deux cents

two thousand deux mille

type le genre

type taper

U

ugly laid(e)

umbrella le parapluie

uncle l'oncle (m.)

under sous, au-dessous

underneath dessous

understand comprendre

underwear les sous-vêtements (m.)

undress se déshabiller

unemployed au chômage

United Kingdom le Royaume-Uni

United States les États-Unis

university l'université (f.)

unlimited illimité(e)

unlocked débloqué(e)

until jusqu'à

update mettre à jour

upstairs en haut

USB cable le câble USB

use employer, se servir de

use l'emploi (m.), l'usage (m.)

usually d'habitude

V

vacancy chambre libre

vacation les vacances (f.)

vacuum l'aspirateur (m.), la balayeuse (Quebec)

valid valable

validate (ticket) composter

valley la vallée

value la valeur

vanilla la vanille

vase le vase

veal le veau

vegan végétalien(ne)

vegetable le légume

vegetarian végétarien(ne)

very très

vest le gilet

victory la victoire

view la vue

village le village

vinegar le vinaigre

visa le visa

visit visiter

vitamin la vitamine

voice la voix

voicemail la messagerie vocale

volleyball le volley

vomit vomir

vote voter

W

waffle le gaufre

wages le salaire

waist la taille

wait for attendre

waiter le serveur

waiting room la salle d'attente

waitress la serveuse

wake up s'éveiller

Wales le Pays-de-Galle

walk se promener, marcher

wallet le portefeuille

walnut la noix

want vouloir, désirer

war la guerre

warm chaud(e)

warn avertir

wash laver

washcloth le gant de toilette, la débarbouillette (Quebec)

washing machine le lave-linge, la laveuse (Quebec)

watch la montre

watch regarder

water l'eau (f.)

water skiing le ski nautique

waterfall la cascade

watermelon le pastèque, le melon d'eau (Quebec)

wave la vague, l'onde (f.)

way le chemin

we nous

weak faible

wealth la richesse

weapon l'arme (f.)

weather le temps

web la toile
web browser le navigateur
webcam la webcam
Wednesday mercredi
week la semaine
weekend le week-end, la fin de semaine (Quebec)
weigh peser
weight le poids
well bien
well done (meat) bien cuite
Welsh gallois(e)
west l'ouest (m.)
what qu'est-ce que, quoi
what time à quelle heure
wheel la roue
wheelchair le fauteuil roulant
when quand
where où
which quel(le)
whiskey le whisky
white blanc(he)
who qui
why pourquoi
wide large
wife la femme
win gagner

wind le vent
wind-surfing la planche à voile
window la fenêtre
window screen la moustiquaire
wine le vin
winter l'hiver (m.)
wire le fil (de fer)
wireless Internet le Wi-Fi
wisdom la sagesse
wisdom teeth les dents (f.) de sagesse
with avec
withdraw retirer
without sans
woman la femme, la dame
wood le bois
wool la laine
word le mot
work travailler; fonctionner
world le monde
worse pire
worst le/la pire
wound la blessure
wrap up envelopper
wrapping paper le papier d'emballage

wrench la clé
wrist le poignet
write écrire
wrong faux, fausse

X
X-rays les radios (f.)

Y
yarn la laine
yawn bailler
year l'an (m.)
yellow jaune
yes oui
yesterday hier
yogurt le yaourt
you (formal) vous
you (informal) tu

you're welcome je vous en prie, de rien, bienvenue (Quebec)
your (formal) votre, vos
your (informal) ton, ta, tes
yours (formal) le vôtre, la vôtre, les vôtres
yours (informal) le tien, la tienne, les tiens, les tiennes

Z
zipper la fermeture éclair, la tirette (Belgium)
zoo le zoo
zucchini la courgette

Index

The words in capitals refer to sections, and the first number that follows (example: p. 129) refers to the page. Otherwise, ALL ENTRIES ARE INDEXED BY ITEM NUMBER.